LEARNING TO HEAL

LEARNING TO HEAL

A Practical Guide for Every Christian

John Coles

Authentic

16 15 14 13 12 11 10   7 6 5 4 3 2 1

This edition first published 2010 by Authentic Media Limited
Milton Keynes
www.authenticmedia.co.uk

British Library Cataloguing-in-Publication Data

A catalogue record for this book is available from the
British Library

ISBN 978-1-85078-857-7

Cover design by Philip Miles
Printed in Great Britain by Cox and Wyman, Reading

Contents

Part 1

The Foundations of the Healing Ministry

Introduction

Everyone knows that to be a Christian involves becoming more like Jesus. My understanding is that this is a process that involves at least three things:

1. Developing the type of relationship with God that Jesus had.
2. Having our lives transformed by the Holy Spirit, so that we increasingly reflect the qualities of purity and holiness that characterised Jesus' life.
3. Learning to minister to others with the same love and power in which Jesus ministered.

In other words, as we become more and more like Jesus, we start to act like Him and to do the kind of things He did. Ministering like Jesus is as much a part of our discipleship as deepening our relationship with God and allowing ourselves to be transformed by the Spirit. They are like the three strands of a rope, designed to be intertwined in such a way that they make our likeness to Jesus as strong and visible as possible. Many believers, however, have spent years focusing only on the first two strands, neglecting the third. The result is that our likeness to Jesus is less than it could be and our witness for Him is less effective than it should be.

It is the desire for us to become 'more like Jesus' in every way possible that underlies this book. In it we will focus on one aspect of the demonstrative ministry of Jesus – that of healing. Why healing? Firstly, because God has taken me on an unexpected journey with this ministry and shown me that it is for ordinary believers in the Church today. Secondly, because so often people respond to those attempting to minister to their physical needs more than they will respond to those trying to 'tell them what they need to hear'.

Healing is a broad topic. It can range from the physical to the emotional; from release from guilt and shame to deliverance from oppressive forces; from the healing of past traumas to present hurts. There is much to learn. But Jesus promised that the Holy Spirit would lead His disciples into an ever deeper understanding and experience of the truth.

> 'But when he, the Spirit of truth, comes, he will guide you into all truth.' (John 16:13)

It is my prayer that as you read this book, the Holy Spirit will lead you further in the truth and enable you to become more like Him.

John Coles
May 2010

1

Rediscovering the Ministry
of Jesus

In many ways my involvement with the ministry of
healing came about by accident. That is to say, it was a
complete surprise to me at least! Healing was not a topic
I had given any thought to during my training for the
ministry and, whilst I believed wholeheartedly in the
biblical account of Jesus' healing miracles, it was not, so
I thought, something that God was still doing today.

Throughout my early growth as a believer and subsequent training for ministry I could have been accurately
described as a conservative evangelical. My first two
curacies were based in what I would call 'mind orient-
ated' churches, working predominantly with young
people and university students, and tertiary educated
adults, first in Reading and then in Bristol. There, the
Gospel appeal was made first and foremost to the intel-
lect and the challenge of believing in Jesus approached
in terms of thought and persuasion. When the moment
came to be a lead pastor for the first time, I took over the
leadership of a liberal, middle-of-the-road Anglican
church with an average Sunday morning congregation

of about fifty elderly people, who were nearly all
over 50!

This was a borough of north London, however, and
not a university area. Something I discovered quickly
was that the intellectual appeal to Christ was not an
approach that worked on 'your average north Lon-
doner!' After labouring hard for some time and seeing
very little fruit, I became frustrated. I wasn't seeing
people come to Christ and having their lives transformed as a result. As this dissatisfaction with my cur-
rent method grew, so did my desperation to see God
intervene. I began to pray, 'Lord, there must be more
than this! How can I become more effective in sharing
your love with others?' This was the beginning of my
journey out of the spiritual wilderness I was living in,
into new and unfamiliar terrain.

Along with my wife, Anne, I spent a good deal of time
praying to God for 'something more' – though in truth,
I was not altogether sure what 'more' would look like.
Then some good friends we had known for years, John
and Eleanor Mumford, who had clearly experienced
some measure of transformation in their own spiritual
lives, began talking to us about the need for a further filling with the power of the Holy Spirit. At the same time
I had read a couple of books on church growth which
also emphasised the need of Holy Spirit empowerment
and so I began praying regularly that God would fill me
afresh with His Spirit or empower me in a new way in
order to become effective in leading people to Christ.

Eventually, I asked John and Eleanor to pray for me
and I remember well experiencing the most wonderful
sense of God's presence I had ever known as He touched
me by the power of His Spirit. At that time I was released
in the gift of tongues and from that moment on, little by
little, my theological perspectives began to change. What

was surprising to me about this encounter was how God awakened in me a desire to see people healed. I had only ever thought that the empowerment of the Holy Spirit was to enable me to be a more effective witness to lead people to Christ. But now I found myself, from time to time, becoming almost overwhelmed with compassion when confronted with a person who was sick. I felt myself desperately wanting, though not yet knowing how, to pray that God would heal them. I had gone looking for power to witness so that I could lead people to Christ, and grow 'my church'; but instead I found God doing something far more profound in my heart.

A Personal Discovery of God's Healing Power

It was not long after this incident that John Mumford invited me to a meeting at Holy Trinity Brompton. The meeting was really for their small group leaders, but a few others were invited along too and I was fortunate to be asked. It was around the time that John Wimber was holding his first public conferences in the UK and another Vineyard pastor, John McClure, was going to be speaking to us.

I took along with me my church warden at the time, because I was keen for others in the church to experience the same touch of the Spirit that I had. During the drive down to Knightsbridge I began to tell her about how God's presence had touched me and the change that it was bringing about in my life. I was surprised to learn that some twenty years previously, she had been similarly 'filled with the Spirit' herself, but because the church she attended at the time did not recognise this as being authentically from God, she had buried the experience and not pursued it. I was glad to know that because I shared my own experience, it reawakened in her a desire to know more of God once again.

The meeting was to be a 'healing meeting' and I told this lady that should the opportunity arise to receive prayer, I would go forward and be prayed for because I had developed a nasty rash on my hand that would not seem to go away. At the meeting, John McClure spoke about God's desire to heal and explained how the gift of the word of knowledge could often be used in this context. After he had finished speaking, he invited members of the team accompanying him to give out any words of knowledge they were receiving from God. Amongst these, someone gave a word about a person who 'has a rash on their hand that is particularly bad at the base of their left thumb.' They had described my ailment perfectly! Those who identified with the words of knowledge being spoken were invited to go out to the front for prayer. I put up my hand and went out. John came over to pray for me and I felt God's power come upon me and my whole body began shaking. From that moment on my rash progressively began to disappear.

I came away from that meeting having learned some important truths. Firstly, I believed in the gift of the word of knowledge and could see how and why it might be used. Secondly, I saw how an ordinary Christian – someone who had come along as part of the Vineyard team – could accurately hear God about the need of someone else. Lastly, I began to see that healing was from God and was, in fact, very much for today.

Proclamation and Demonstration

Jesus was committed not only to proclaiming the good news of God's kingdom and love through His words –

by preaching it to others – but also to demonstrating it. He showed people the reality of that kingdom and its ability to invade our world by bringing healing to the sick and freedom to the oppressed. Matthew 9:35 clearly indicates the connection and balance between these two essential elements:

> 'Jesus went through all the towns and villages, teaching in their synagogues, preaching the good news of the kingdom and healing every disease and sickness.'

The motivation behind Jesus' healings was His compassion. Healing was a natural expression of the outpouring of God's love into people's lives.

> 'When Jesus . . . saw a large crowd, he had compassion on them and healed their sick.' (Matt. 14:14)

As John Wimber used to say, Jesus was a 'word-worker'. His words proclaimed the reality of the kingdom of God and His works demonstrated the reality of it. As I continued on my own journey, I began to see more and more how this dynamic of the kingdom held true for every believer. Every Christian is called to learn to minister like this.

Through the life of Jesus as told in the gospels there is a natural progression in the training and sending out of more and more workers into the harvest field. We see that,

- First, Jesus Himself did this work wherever He went:

> 'So he travelled throughout Galilee, preaching in their synagogues and driving out demons.' (Mark 1:39)

- Then Jesus chose twelve others in order to train them. They were to be with Him wherever He went, watching Him and learning from Him how He preached and brought healing to the oppressed:

  'He appointed twelve – designating them apostles – that they might be with him and that he might send them out to preach and to have authority to drive out demons.' (Mark 3:14–15)

- When the time was right, Jesus sent out those He had been training to minister to others in the same way that they had seen and heard Him minister:

  'When Jesus had called the Twelve together, he gave them power and authority to drive out all demons and to cure diseases and he sent them out to preach the kingdom of God and to heal the sick.' (Luke 9:1–2)

- Later, Jesus commissioned a second wave of trainees to do the same thing:

  'After this the Lord appointed seventy-two others and sent them two by two ahead of him to every town and place where he was about to go . . . Heal the sick who are there and tell them, "The kingdom of God is near you."' (Luke 10:1,9)

- Finally, Jesus entrusted to those He had trained in His lifetime the responsibility of teaching and training subsequent generations of believers to do exactly the same things:

  'Therefore go and make disciples of all nations, baptizing them in the name of the Father and of the

> Son and of the Holy Spirit, and teaching them to
> obey everything I have commanded you.' (Matt.
> 28:19–20)

Through my experiences these scriptures came alive to
me in a way that I had previously missed. I realised that
Jesus' command to go into all the world and make disciples must have included the command to heal, since this
is what He had invested so much time into training His
disciples to do. They were to spread the good news of
the kingdom not only by proclaiming it, but also by
demonstrating it through praying for the sick to be healed
and the oppressed to be set free.

It is clear that in the New Testament Church this ministry was not just exercised by the apostles (the first
twelve disciples), but they were 'prototype' disciples
who were setting a pattern for all future believers of
Jesus. There are named and unnamed Christians who
were not part of the original twelve or seventy-two who
were given the same ministry:

> 'So Paul and Barnabas spent considerable time there,
> speaking boldly for the Lord, who confirmed the mes-
> sage of his grace by enabling them to do miraculous
> signs and wonders.' (Acts 14:3)

> 'This salvation, which was first announced by the Lord,
> was confirmed to us by those who heard him. God also
> testified to it by signs, wonders and various miracles,
> and gifts of the Holy Spirit distributed according to his
> will.' (Heb. 2:3–4)

It seems clear that it was Jesus' intention that the ministry of healing the sick should be a natural part of every
Christian's life.

'And these signs will accompany those who believe . . .
they will place their hands on sick people, and they will
get well.' (Mark 16:17–18)

There is nothing in Scripture that suggests either that
this commission was reserved purely for the first disciples or that it would be rescinded at some point in the
future. The command to demonstrate the reality of
God's kingdom through healing, therefore, is a command to all Christians in all places at all times.

Francis McNutt writes in his book *Power to Heal* that,
'It's only when thousands of ministers are praying for
the sick that people will begin to regard the healing ministry as ordinary. Only then will the healer be regarded
neither as an object of scorn, nor as a subject for worship.'

We are fortunate to live in an age when God is restor-
ing this type of 'every member ministry' not just to
church ministers, but to every Christian believer who is
willing to learn about it. It is not an optional extra for a
few privileged or highly spiritual Christians; it is becoming an integral part of the life and ministry of many ordinary Christians. As a consequence healing ministry is
gaining visibility and credibility even in the Western
world.

2

The Conflict of Two Kingdoms

Around one year after my personal healing experience we were able to host a visiting Vineyard pastor at our church. This was shortly after John Wimber's first public conferences in the UK at Westminster Central Hall, during the autumn of 1984. Bob Craine, one of Wimber's associates on this trip, was pastor of another Californian Vineyard and he arrived with a team of people to spend the weekend with us.

We put on a full programme of events to give Bob plenty of opportunity to minister. He preached several times over the weekend and each time, after he'd spoken, his team had various words of knowledge for people and proceeded to pray for them. Such 'body ministry' may now seem routine in many quarters of the Church – though not all – but back then it brought something of a revelation to me. I suddenly saw a new way of doing church that wasn't focused on the leaders and where the ministry didn't have to come from 'the front'. It was fantastic to see small groups of people all over the building ministering to each other with the grace, love and healing power of God. I knew then that this was how I wanted to 'do church' every week – that whenever God's people gathered together, there would be times of praying for one another, so that people left the building changed by a real, tangible encounter with Him. Sometimes that prayer might be for healing, sometimes it would be for other things, but it would most definitely not be driven from the front. Everyone could be involved.

What I had seen was a microcosm of the kingdom of God in action. God always intended for His reign to be established – in other words, for Heaven to be brought to Earth – by ordinary believers exercising their faith and acting on His Word. Throughout Jesus' teaching we clearly see this theme of inclusivity, with every believer vitally involved in kingdom action. Nowhere do we see Jesus suggesting that only a few specially anointed people can pray for others and expect to see healing or other kinds of supernatural manifestation. The supernatural is intended to be a *natural* part of every believer's life.

Jesus' Central Theme

The kingdom of God breaking out and having a supernatural impact wherever it touches people was a constant theme of Jesus' teaching. In fact, it was His *central* theme. He talked constantly about God's kingdom, by which He meant the present rule and reign of a good God, and emphasised that it could be experienced, but also ministered, by anyone who believed and could exercise faith. It formed the basis for His first sermon (Mark 1:14) during which He proclaimed, *'The time has come, the kingdom of God is near.'* It featured in nearly all of His parables: *'The kingdom of heaven is like . . .'* and it was central to the prayer that He taught us to pray: *'Your kingdom come, on earth as it is in heaven.'*

Jesus also showed us how we are to practice kingdom ministry. He spoke about 'hearing' and 'seeing' what the Father was doing and said He could do only what the Father showed Him to do, and say what the Father told Him to say. This wasn't a limiting factor for Jesus, rather it was releasing! He was modelling for us a pattern for life and ministry that focuses on listening carefully to God – a ministry empowered by His presence. This is what the rule and reign of God looks like on earth. Jesus showed us that we are first to pray and listen to God, then enact His will and bring the reality of Heaven to Earth. The book of Revelation reveals Heaven as a place where there is no pain, no tears or mourning, and an absence of death. The sickness, suffering and decay that characterises our earthly lives is eradicated. So it is reasonable to expect that as ordinary believers establish the rule and reign of God on Earth, healing will be an essential part of the equation. Healing and wholeness is a natural part of God's kingdom expressed on the Earth.

The Nature of the Kingdom

Isaiah prophesied that the 'Good News' that God was alive, powerful and reigning would be the message and mandate of the Messianic Servant of God when He came, and also that of His followers:

> 'How beautiful on the mountains are the feet of those who bring good news, who proclaim peace, who bring good tidings, who proclaim salvation, who say to Zion, "Your God reigns!"' (Isa. 52:7)

This kingdom was going to be unlike any other, because it would know no boundaries. It was not to be exclusively for those of a particular nationality (e.g. the Jews) or located in a particular place (e.g. Israel) – both of which were shocking statements for Jesus' Jewish audience. Instead, God's kingdom would be open to any and all who were willing to receive God's rule in their lives.

The same is still true today. God's kingdom is a spiritual reality that anyone can enter if they are born again by the Holy Spirit.

> 'Jesus answered, "I tell you the truth, no one can enter the kingdom of God unless he is born of water and the Spirit. Flesh gives birth to flesh, but the Spirit gives birth to spirit.' (John 3:5–6)

As Jesus went around preaching the good news, He introduced the key issues of the immediacy, goodness and accessibility of the kingdom:

> '"The time has come," he said. "The kingdom of God is near. Repent and believe the good news!"' (Mark 1:15)

Jesus revealed to us the very nature of God's kingdom and, importantly, the fact that it cannot be contained. God is moving everywhere by the power of His Holy Spirit and His plan was always to 'invest' His presence in ordinary believers so that they could be used powerfully to demonstrate His rule. Wherever Jesus' followers are prepared to step out in faith and obedience, the power of the kingdom 'spills out' and touches people and situations in remarkable ways.

In the early days of our church, when we had just begun to establish house groups, I wanted there to be a spiritual 'DNA' built into these gatherings which meant that worship, Bible study and the use of the gifts of the Spirit would be a natural part of the proceedings. So whenever we met, in as unforced a way as possible, we would ask God to release the gifts in our midst and wait on Him to see what would happen. Early on, in one such gathering, one of the group members said, 'I think there is someone here who has a problem with their left ear.' Someone else in the room responded, explaining that they had suffered from an ongoing problem with discharge in their left ear all their life, which frequently impeded their hearing. The whole group gathered around the lady with the problem and prayed. She was healed that day and has never suffered with the problem since.

Since then there have been many similar incidences too numerous to recount. This underlines to me the fact that not only will God use ordinary members of the church to bring healing, but He will do it anywhere at any time, without the need for a special meeting or a visiting speaker. God's kingdom is meant to function naturally and organically as ordinary Christians seek His face and act on the Spirit's prompting. The only requirement is that we focus our energy on God's agenda rather than our own.

> 'But seek first his kingdom and his righteousness, and all these things will be given to you as well.' (Matt. 6:33)

The Kingdom of Darkness

This of course begs certain questions: if God's kingdom is so present in the world in the lives of believers, why do so many people still suffer from sickness? And of those who are prayed for, why do many still remain unhealed?

The first of these questions is more straightforward to answer than the second. Many people will point to sickness and suffering as 'evidence' that, contrary to Jesus' teaching, God is either not *good* or not present. We have heard the mantra, 'Why would God allow all this suffering?' hundreds of times. The problem that most people have is that they neither experience the reality of the kind rule and reign of God in their lives, nor know of the goodness of God. Why not? The Bible's answer is clear and unequivocal:

> 'The whole world is under the control of the evil one.' (1 John 5:19)

Elsewhere we read that,

> 'The devil, or Satan . . . leads the whole world astray.' (Rev. 12:9)

And in one of His parables about the kingdom, Jesus answers the question about how there can be so much evil in a world created by a good God:

> 'The owner's servants came to him and said, "Sir, didn't you sow good seed in your field? Where then did the weeds come from?" **"An enemy did this"** he replied.' (Matt. 13:27–8)

The heart of the problem is that we live in a fallen world subject to decay and destruction, overseen by a self-appointed enemy of God, 'the devil'. His deliberate aim is to destroy the lives of human beings by destroying their relationship with God and leading them in self-destructive patterns of belief and behaviour, otherwise known as sin. As a consequence, most people live most of their lives unaware of the goodness of God, under a blanket of spiritual ignorance. The Bible even talks of there being two kingdoms locked in a conflict that rages all around us as the devil pursues his ultimate aim of preventing people from recognizing the love of God and the possibility of Him reigning supernaturally in their lives. The spiritual blindness at work in the earth militates against even the very *knowledge* of God's existence.

> 'The god of this age has blinded the minds of unbelievers, so that they cannot see the light of the gospel of the glory of Christ, who is the image of God.' (2 Cor. 4:4)

The devil exercises his scheming and destructive rule over everyone born into the world and together with his malicious army of demons is deeply opposed to everything Jesus Christ and His followers stand for. This is why the Bible instructs believers to,

> 'Put on the full armour of God so that you can take your stand against the devil's schemes. For our struggle is not against flesh and blood, but against the rulers, against the authorities, against the powers of this dark world and against the spiritual forces of evil in the heavenly realms.' (Eph. 6:11–12)

A member of my church once related the following story to me which illustrates the reality of our conflict with evil forces. Doug would occasionally give a colleague a lift to work in the morning. One day this man complained of an intense pain in his knee. He had been walking with a limp for some time, but now the pain had worsened. Doug stepped out in faith and said, 'Can I pray for you then? Because I believe Jesus can heal it.' His work colleague agreed and Doug prayed. The next day Doug asked the man how his knee was, but was told it didn't seem to be any better. Undeterred, Doug asked if he could pray once again. This time he felt the Holy Spirit prompt him to pray against a curse that had been spoken over the man and he did so.

The next day, Doug noticed his colleague walking normally, without a limp, going up a flight of stairs in their offices. The man told Doug that his pain had completely disappeared and he was now able to walk normally. He also explained that before leaving his home country in Africa to come and work in London, he'd had a major argument with some members of his family. It seemed that in their anger they had (deliberately or inadvertently) cursed him which had resulted in his limp and subsequent knee pain.

Often demonic influences in a person's life will operate in a much less obvious fashion than on this man – but they are just as real. I don't want to over-focus on demonic activity, because I believe doing so can lead to an unhealthy preoccupation with evil that has a counterproductive effect – causing us to lose sight of God's overwhelming ability and power to deal with it. But it is helpful for us to understand how the devil continually tries to usurp God's authority, involving human beings in the process, and what the consequences are whenever he succeeds. These consequences are summarised below.

1. Deception

Under the prevailing spiritual blindness, people are deceived into believing they are free when in reality they are not. They are unable to think clearly or see the truth about God, or themselves

> 'The god of this age has blinded the minds of unbelievers, so that they cannot see the light of the gospel of the glory of Christ, who is the image of God.' (2 Cor. 4:4)

2. Dominion of sin

Sin has a power over our lives which it is humanly impossible to escape from and it has immediate and eternal consequences:

> 'Whoever believes in him is not condemned, but whoever does not believe stands condemned already because he has not believed in the name of God's one and only Son.' (John 3:18)

> 'Jesus replied, "I tell you the truth, everyone who sins is a slave to sin."' (John 8:34)

3. Disease

The biblical view of the origin of sickness is that it is 'from the enemy'. But this doesn't mean that every single sickness is a result of a demonic attack. It simply means that the environment we live in is so affected by the enemy that we no longer experience the presence of God in natural good health.

The difference between our future experience of Heaven and our present environment on Earth is that the enemy will not be present, nor have any effect, in the new creation. Heaven is a sickness-free-zone because it is enemy free. This is clear from the biblical picture of Heaven:

> 'He will wipe every tear from their eyes. There will be no more death or mourning or crying or pain, for the old order of things has passed away.' (Rev. 21:4)

4. *Demonisation*

Sometimes the enemy's work results in serious physical symptoms, sometimes in emotional disturbance, and sometimes in behavioural or social problems. The enemy never plays fair. Although an ungodly life seems to invite his further assault, there are times when even the most godly people are assaulted to the point of despair by demonic attack through no fault of their own:

> 'So Satan went out from the presence of the LORD and afflicted Job.' (Job 2:7)

The enemy can also exercise his rule through demonic beings who are constantly seeking to assault, oppress and invade people, always with the intention of destroying their lives:

> 'Your enemy the devil prowls around like a roaring lion looking for someone to devour.' (1 Pet. 5:8)

5. *Division*

The increasing breakdown of society and the seemingly irreconcilable divisions in the nuclear family, between the generations, in local communities, in nations, and internationally, all originate from the enemy's destructive desires. It was never God's intention that we should experience such pain and loneliness in interpersonal or international relationships. The dividing wall separating people from each other has come from the enemy and can only be broken by the power of the Lord Jesus:

> For Christ himself is our peace, who . . . has destroyed the barrier, the dividing wall of hostility . . . His purpose

> was to create in himself one new man out of the two,
> thus making peace . . .' (Eph. 2:14–15)

Jesus was always welcoming people that other religious people would normally have rejected into the new community of love that He was forming with his disciples.

6. Disaster

Throughout history 'natural disasters' have plagued, and will continue to plague human life. These often sudden, unexpected and life-destroying events bring a challenge to many who believe in God's providential oversight of life on planet earth. That is particularly true in the Western world, where education and technology have given us the false impression that human beings can control their environment and their destiny. To discover this is not the case comes as a traumatic shock, and in today's culture of culpability it is God who would have to take the blame. For many this picture of God allowing such injustice, in which the innocent suffer, is intolerable and consequentially they turn their backs on the only One who could save from these very things.

> 'When you hear of wars and rumours of wars, do not be
> alarmed. Such things must happen, but the end is still to
> come. Nation will rise against nation, and kingdom
> against kingdom. There will be earthquakes in various
> places, and famines. These are the beginning of birth
> pains.' (Mark 13:7-8)

The Bible's view of such things is that they belong only to this fallen world and in the newly recreated Heaven and Earth there will be complete harmony between human beings and their environment (Isa. 11:6).

7. Death

Death too comes as a result of the fall and is seen to be the last enemy of human beings. It has been overcome through the death and resurrection victory of Jesus and new and eternally indestructible life will be given to all in Christ when He returns:

> 'For since death came through a man, the resurrection of the dead comes also through a man . . . The last enemy to be destroyed is death.' (1 Cor. 15:21,26)

The assurance of a future life beyond the grave can be received now through faith in Jesus:

> 'Jesus said to her, "I am the resurrection and the life. Anyone who believes in me will live, even though they die; and whoever lives by believing in me will never die."' (John 11:25–26 TNIV)

All these things, marks of the enemy's work, are things that Jesus came to overcome. This is what His ministry was all about and what He spent His time doing. The gospels are full of stories of how He overcame the destructive work of the enemy in each of these areas. In addition, 1 John 3:8 assures us of Christ's power and commitment to overturn *all* the work of the enemy:

> 'The reason the Son of God appeared was to destroy the devil's work.' (1 John 3:8)

The table shows how, at every point, the power of God's kingdom overcomes the power of the kingdom of darkness, with a Bible story describing what that meant for individuals suffering from each sort of consequence of the fall:

Kingdom of Darkness	Kingdom of God
Deception	Truth and Light E.g. John 3:21 – for everyone; John 8:32–44 – for religious people
Dominion of sin	Forgiveness and Salvation E.g. Mark 2:5 – the paralysed man; Luke 19:9 – Zacchaeus
Disease	Healing E.g. Mark 10:52 – blind Bartimaeus; Matt. 8:16 – for everyone
Demonisation	Deliverance E.g. Matt. 12:22 – blind/mute man; Mark 5 – man with legions of demons
Division	Life and Community E.g. Mark 2:14 – Levi, a tax collector; Luke 7:37 – the prostitute
Disaster	Miracles E.g. Mark 4:39 – stilling the storm; Matt. 14:21 – feeding the 5,000
Death	Resurrection E.g. John 11:44 – Lazarus; Luke 7:15 – the widow's son

The Ultimate Victory of God's Kingdom

We see that the kingdom of God overthrows the kingdom of darkness at every point. Jesus came to push back
the boundaries of darkness and establish God's sovereign rule. Not only in His life and ministry did He
overcome the work of the enemy in the lives of individuals He encountered, but He won the decisive victory
for us all through His death on the cross.

> 'God forgave us all our sins, having cancelled the writ-
> ten code, with its regulations, that was against us and
> that stood opposed to us; he took it away, nailing it to the
> cross. And having disarmed the powers and authorities,
> he made a public spectacle of them, triumphing over
> them by the cross.' (Col. 2:13–15)

On the cross Jesus inflicted a death-blow upon the enemy.
Though strong, he is now bound and his power is curbed
(Matt. 12.29). His doom is sealed and the final victory of
Jesus over all the power of the enemy is now in sight:

> 'The end will come, when Christ hands over the king-
> dom to God the Father after he has destroyed all domin-
> ion, authority and power. For he must reign until he has
> put all his enemies under his feet. The last enemy to be
> destroyed is death.' (1 Cor. 15:24–26)

It is apparent that in one sense the kingdom of God has
come already. When Jesus cast out demons he could say,
*'But if I drive out demons by the Spirit of God, then the
kingdom of God has come upon you'* (Matt. 12:28). Yet, in
another sense the kingdom of God has not yet come. At
the Last Supper Jesus spoke of the complete reign of
God as something still in the future:

'For I tell you I will not drink again of the fruit of the vine until the kingdom of God comes.' (Luke 22:18)

This fullness of the kingdom of God will be established when the Lord Jesus returns. That is why the Bible finishes with a prayer *'Come, Lord Jesus'* expressing both our longing for Him and our longing for an end to all the destructive activity of the enemy (Rev. 22:20). In a sense we live now in the 'in between times'. The power of the present ruler of this world has been broken and something of the power of the next world, of Heaven itself, has broken in. This is really the answer to the second question that was asked earlier: why is it that some who are prayed for are not healed? Whilst acknowledging that we do not know why some are healed and others are not, we know that we are not yet experiencing the fullness of God's kingdom. In these 'in between' times not everyone we pray for will be healed. Nevertheless, every time we do see someone saved, healed or delivered we are seeing something more of that glorious future which one day everyone in Christ will experience. These things are signs of the kingdom and should impart faith to us that even more can happen if we are faithful to pray, *'Your kingdom come, your will be done on earth as it is in heaven'* (Matt. 6:9–10).

If being a Christian involves becoming more like Jesus and learning to minister like Him, then every Christian needs to learn how to *bring* the kingdom of God into the lives of others. Doing so will involve us overcoming the work of the enemy in these same areas that Jesus did. We do this both through our proclamation of the simple gospel truth that *'our God reigns'* (Isa. 52:7) and through learning to pray for, expect, and minister in powerful signs and wonders at the same time: *'For the kingdom of God is not a matter of talk but of power'* (1 Cor. 4:20).

How does one go about this? We can make a start by being sensitive to the voice of the Holy Spirit and daring to ask individuals we meet if we can pray for them as God prompts us. Or we can join with others who are similarly interested in learning about healing. When Anne and I were first learning about healing we announced to the church that we were going to hold a series of six seminars fortnightly on Saturday mornings for anyone similarly interested. I wasn't really confident that the little I knew would help anyone, so I bought a set of John Wimber's teaching tapes from the Vineyard and we listened to one each week. After discussion we tried to put what we had learnt into practice praying for anyone who was sick, and expecting God to bring healing. I was deliberately trying to create a positive learning environment where it was possible for people to take steps of faith in this area of discipleship, without being criticised by others in the church who either thought that healing had died out with the end of the apostolic period, or that these new Christians (as some of them were) were too immature to learn about healing. I remember the anxiety in one of the first 'practicals' when I asked God to give some words of knowledge about people who needed healing. But one young man, new to this whole idea, said he thought there was someone with a serious rash under their right armpit. 'In a room of only 16 people is that possible?' I thought. Imagine my delight when someone said, 'That's me – please pray for me!' We did, and from that day the rash began to disappear as the Lord healed her. I believe being in this sort of 'safe' learning environment is the best way for most of us to learn this ministry.

More recently we discovered another initiative designed to help people learn how to minister to others on the streets. Taking inspiration from Mark Marx of

Coleraine Vineyard in Northern Ireland (see www.out-there.org), in the spring of 2008 we began to take a team out onto the busy highroad of our North London community and took the initiative of asking people if they would like to receive prayer for healing. This was not something that even I would have dared to do alone, but doing it in a team with others gave us all the courage to 'have a go'. It is interesting in this context that Jesus sent out the first disciples (learners) in pairs. He must have realised that doing this alone would be difficult for those first adventurous apostles. The response has been amazing. People are much more willing to be prayed for than we might think.

I recall one occasion when I was travelling to one of our prayer locations by bus. I noticed the lady sitting next to me was wearing a badge saying, 'Best Mum in the World'. I'm not normally talkative on buses, but I struck up a conversation with her, during which she told me that her daughter was ill in hospital. I found myself asking her if I could pray for her there and then on the bus. She agreed and I prayed that the Lord would embrace her and her daughter with His love. As I did so, it was as if Heaven came down. There was a very real sense of the presence of God on that bus and of His overwhelming love for this lady. Afterwards she looked at me with wide open eyes, clearly touched by the experience, and just kept repeating the words 'thank you!' over and over.

It's much easier to say to someone, 'Can I pray for your need?' than it is to ask, 'Can I talk to you about Jesus?' Rather than trying to convince people with words, Jesus more often acted to bring the reality of the supernatural to bear in a person's life. Once we have prayed for someone and they have been touched by the love of God, it frequently opens the door for us to speak to them freely about Jesus. This has been our experience with the 'healing on the streets' ministry. Jesus said we should go and proclaim the kingdom and heal the sick. As people are touched and healed, it results in many more opportunities to share our message of hope. Jesus always invited people to believe in Him, but if they couldn't believe because of what He was saying, then He invited them to believe on the basis of what He was doing.

Dave is typical of someone who has come to faith like this. He is one of those we have come to call 'our friends from the benches'. Our prayer point has a number of benches around it which we have discovered are a gathering place for a number of homeless people. Many of these people are also addicts, whose lives are being destroyed by the enemy. We realised we couldn't just say to them 'God bless you,' when they were cold and hungry, so as well as offering to pray for them we always offer coffee or a burger, or try to meet other immediate needs such as buying woolly hats and gloves for them in the winter. When we met Dave he was sleeping in a garage and estimated that he had been drinking about 45 units of alcohol a day for two months. His first encounter with the team was on a cold November morning after a friend of his said, 'I know where we can get a free cup of coffee.'

He took Dave to our prayer point and, sure enough, as well as prayer, the coffee turned up. Dave and his friend were then invited for lunch in a burger restaurant with the team after they had packed up. Both men were invited to St Barnabas that Sunday. 'I was blown away,' Dave said. 'There's something about that church – the presence there.' After his second visit to church, Dave read the Bible all night and made a snap decision to stop drinking the following morning. Recognising that this could endanger Dave's life, a member of the healing team took him to hospital for medication and checked up on him throughout the 'detox' process. On Christmas Day he decided to wholeheartedly give his life to Jesus. 'The thing about being an addict is that you can't press your "stop" button,' he explained. 'But it was like someone pressed it for me. God gave me my life back, so all I could do was give Him mine: heart, body, soul and mind.' On the same day he was literally handed the keys to a flat by a member of the team he had never met before. This person had a spare room in his flat and heard that Dave might need it. Dave is a carpenter by trade and is now a valuable full time volunteer on the maintenance team in the church.

As well as creating many more opportunities to speak to people about Jesus, this kind of ministry has allowed us to reach a much wider cross section of our community. Churches that embrace healing ministry will see a much broader spectrum of society coming to Christ. As our own church prays on the streets we are in touch with 'street people' – the homeless, drug addicts – that we never touched before. During the last year many of these have come to a real faith in Christ. Previously our church programmes didn't include the needs of such people, but through the healing ministry God has helped us to reach out to them and offer help.

Because we live in this 'in between' time, we will probably discover that not all the people we pray for will get healed. On these occasions we, and those we have prayed for, are reassured of God's love and His power to heal by our understanding that the kingdom is both here now, and at the same time not yet fully here. It is vital we grasp this truth if we are to persevere when the going is difficult. If we don't grasp this now-not-yet tension we are likely to fall into one of two traps. First we might promise too much: 'It's all possible now if you believe properly.' The consequence of this is often that the chronically sick give up and leave our churches because their hopes are raised and dashed so many times that they lose heart. Second, we can give up because we are not seeing the results we want and pray for, and its easier to go back to a cessationist view, where you expect nothing and get nothing this side of Jesus' return.

Nevertheless, at all times, whether we are seeing great fruit in ministering healing or not, the priority of those who live in the kingdom of God remains the same: to continue to reach out to the lost, hurting and broken just as Jesus did, and to usher in the rule and reign of His kingdom.

3

Authority and Power

Some years ago, I was working at my desk in the church office when I twisted my back as I was getting up. I was immediately in excruciating pain – so much so that I could only crawl out of my office on all fours! My secretary spotted me crawling along and, understandably, asked me if I was alright. She quickly decided that I was in so much pain that she should call an ambulance and in due course one arrived and I was taken to hospital.

After being examined by a doctor I was told I had probably trapped a nerve and that I would have to spend the next 6 weeks lying on my back at home. I was released to go still unable to move without experiencing searing pain. The paramedics had to carry me into the house on a stretcher and helped find an appropriate 'spot' to place me on the sitting room floor. They also told me that I would have to spend the next few weeks here – lying on the floor – while my muscles gradually came out of spasm and began to release the trapped nerve. It wasn't a very happy prognosis to say the least!

The following day, however, a friend came to visit me, when I told him my predicament and asked him if he could come and pray for me. As he prayed for me I felt a gentle warmth, and he then asked if I could try and get up from my mat. I gingerly rolled over and levered myself onto my haunches, surprised at how little pain I felt. I gradually stood and tentatively began to twist and turn my torso, movements which led me to faint the day before. The residual pain rapidly subsided and after an hour I was almost completely pain free. My wife was almost as surprised as I was when she returned from an evening meeting to find me able to greet her standing up rather than prostrate on the floor. I was extremely thankful to God and to this faithful friend for praying. When I returned to the hospital for a follow up consultation some time later the doctor was equally surprised when I told him of my recovery. After examining me he pondered aloud, 'How did you get better so quickly?' I told him that I had experienced the power of God in healing as a friend had prayed for me. The doctor examined me once more and decided that I was in fact completely well. In the end he added to my medical record that I had been 'healed by faith'!

Since then, God has manifest His power to me numerous times. Incidentally, He has used me frequently to minister healing to others who have bad backs since this experience. What has become clear to me through such experiences is this: God can and will use ordinary Christians as conduits of His power to touch others miraculously. But, for ordinary Christians to be involved in healing ministry they need to understand two foundational truths:

1. That God gives them the authority to carry out this ministry.
2. That it is the Holy Spirit who empowers them for this ministry.

The friend who prayed for me that day understood this and, coupled with an expectancy of seeing God move, was effective in ministering God's healing power to me.

How do we understand the distinction between authority and power, and why is it important?

There are places in the Bible where the word 'authority' implies 'power' and other passages where the word 'power' also implies 'authority'. But there are also verses of Scripture where the two words are used together, so that each must mean something different. Witnesses to Jesus' ministry on Earth saw Him using both:

> 'All the people were amazed and said to each other, "What is this teaching? With authority and power he gives orders to evil spirits and they come out!"' (Luke 4:36)

The word authority comes from the Greek *exousia*. It implies having the *right* to do something. For example, a policeman in uniform bears as insignia of authority which gives him the right to apprehend members of the public who are behaving unlawfully. The word *power* comes from the Greek *dunamis* and implies having the *ability* to do something. For example, a prison officer holding a set of keys for a cell has not only the authority, but also the power to contain or release a prisoner.

To have authority but no power to exercise it would be humiliating. But equally, to possess power without being authorised to use it would be dangerous. Jesus showed us how authority and power are to be held together in balanced tension. He knew that He had both the authority and the power to bring healing to the sick. If we are to practise healing ministry like Jesus, then so must we.

Authority

Jesus' authority over everything in the created order flowed out from living under God's authority in His own life. Because Jesus was born without sin – in effect He was the second Adam – He regained the authority that God entrusted to the first human beings made in His image:

> 'Then God said, "Let us make man in our image, in our likeness, and let them rule over the fish of the sea and the birds of the air, over the livestock, over all the earth, and over all the creatures that move along the ground."' (Gen. 1:26)

It seems evident from these verses that human beings were intended to act as God's vice-regents on Earth, exercising their dominion in properly caring for the environment in which God placed them. When man rebelled against God's authority, he lost both the right to, and the understanding of how to, exercise this authority. We no longer *know* how to exercise our godly authority as God's vice-regents, but in Christ that authority is restored to us.

Jesus, who never rebelled against God's authority, naturally had absolute godly authority and a God-given right to heal the sick. We regain our authority once we are born again into a renewed relationship with God. Here we find both godly authority and access to new spiritual power. John 1:12 confirms that anyone who receives Christ and believes in His name is given the 'right' to become a 'child of God'. The word translated 'right' in this passage is *exousia*. In other words, our lost authority is restored in Christ. Authority is part of our birthright as believers. John 1:12 could equally be translated, '*He gave to them the **authority of** children of God*'.

So in Christ the rightful place of human beings in and over the rest of creation is restored. Jesus made this clear when He sent His disciples ahead of Him into the surrounding towns and villages:

> 'When Jesus had called the Twelve together, he gave them power and **authority** to drive out all demons and to cure diseases.' (Luke 9:1)

Jesus expected that His disciples would emulate His ministry and do all of the things He Himself did. So He commissioned them and made them aware that they possessed the same level of authority as Him. It must have been a moment of immense revelation as Jesus told them, in so many words, 'Don't you realise? This is what you were born for! Go and do what I've been doing.' Jesus says the same to us today. He wants each of us to know that we too have been given the same authority to exercise. It is the main reason why we are not simply caught up to Heaven as soon as we are saved – we have a job to do on Earth, exercising our godly authority as He intended! The Bible says that Jesus was the 'first born among many'. We are the many – the children of God designed to act in the same way as Christ Himself.

God may use various means in order to assure us of this God-given authority. He will speak to us about it through the Bible and He will frequently encourage us to pray about various issues so that we invite Him to display His power through us. With regard to the healing ministry specifically, God often seems to use the process of commissioning and authorizing in a public meeting. A single moment like this can release a lifetime's awareness of authority for some. For others there may need to be a series of such 'authorisations' before the penny drops. Sometimes people are slow to respond to God's promptings because they are bound by past negative teaching about the ministry of the Holy Spirit and healing in particular, so we will need to be set free from such restrictions before we truly understand our authority to heal the sick.

Though Jesus knew He had been given a 'general' authority to go out and heal the sick, He was also dependent, moment by moment, on receiving instructions from the Father regarding when and how He was to engage in this ministry. This was true both of what He said and when He said it . . .

> 'For I did not speak of my own accord, but the Father who sent me commanded me what to say and how to say it.' (John 12:49)

. . . and of when and how He ministered healing:

> 'Jesus gave them this answer: "I tell you the truth, the Son can do nothing by himself; he can do only what he sees his Father doing."' (John 5:19)

This is an interesting case in point. Jesus said these words when He went to the Pool of Bethesda. There were many sick people sitting around the pool, but He only healed one paralyzed man. It seems to be the case that this was the one person the Father had pointed out to Jesus as being ready at that moment.

If we are to exercise our God-given authority in the same way that Jesus did and be used effectively in healing ministry, we need to cultivate lives similarly consecrated in obedience to God. We need to become as committed to holiness as Jesus was and as sensitive to the

Father's daily prompting in ministry. One of the reasons for our relative ineffectiveness in ministry, compared to Jesus, is that we are often consumed with our own needs and prayer requests and relatively ignorant of what is on God's heart. Our lack of clearly hearing and obeying God's will in our lives stifles our effectiveness.

This sensitivity to the prompting of the Father is also something we need to cultivate if we are not to be exhausted by the constant and pressing needs which we will face as we engage in healing ministry. On one occasion we are told that Jesus insisted in moving on, even when there were still people not healed:

> 'At daybreak Jesus went out to a solitary place. The people were looking for him and when they came to where he was, they tried to keep him from leaving them. But he said, "I must preach the good news of the kingdom of God to the other towns also, because that is why I was sent."' (Luke 4:42–43)

Sometimes, the expressed needs of people are what we must focus our time and energy on. But sometimes we need to learn to stop. This is where learning to obey God is more important than responding to people clamouring for our attention.

Power

Even though Jesus knew Himself to be the Son of God from early in His life, and therefore must have known the authority that God had given Him to be His co-regent on Earth, we don't read of Him exercising any supernatural ministry until after He was anointed with the power of the Holy Spirit following His baptism.

> 'God anointed Jesus of Nazareth with the Holy Spirit
> and power, and . . . he went around doing good and
> healing all who were under the power of the devil,
> because God was with him.' (Acts 10:38)

From this, we understand that we have a need for being
empowered by the Spirit as well as being *authorised* as
a child of God. This empowering, as seen in Christ's
ministry and the acts of the Apostles, enables a bold
proclamation of the gospel with signs and wonders
accompanying. Sometimes Christians think that Jesus
performed all His miraculous healings as a result of
being divine – i.e. the incarnate second Person of the
Trinity. But it's quite possible to argue that Jesus was
able to heal the sick because He was a human being fulfilled with the power of the Spirit. Right at the start of
His ministry Jesus seems to acknowledge this, rather
than His divine nature, as the source of His power when
He reads from the prophet Isaiah in the synagogue:

> 'The **Spirit of the Lord** is on me, because he has anoin-
> ted me to preach good news to the poor. He has sent me
> to proclaim freedom for the prisoners and recovery of
> sight for the blind, to release the oppressed, to proclaim
> the year of the Lord's favour.' (Luke 4:18–19)

This has been recognised by numerous theologians in the
past, such as R.A. Torrey who wrote, 'Jesus Christ obtained
power for his divine works not by His inherent divinity,
but by his anointing through the Holy Spirit. He was subject to the same conditions of power as other men.'

If Jesus had healed the sick only because He was
divine, then there would be no possibility of the healing
ministry being part of today's Church (let alone the
Apostolic Church). But if Jesus was a human being,

empowered by the Spirit for this ministry, then there is the possibility that any of His followers might be empowered for a similar ministry. This, in fact, is exactly what Jesus was doing when He released the disciples to go into the villages ahead of Him (Luke 9:1). Scripture also makes clear that this empowering comes from the Holy Spirit:

> 'But you will receive **power** when the Holy Spirit comes on you.' (Acts 1:8)

If we are to be used by God in ministry – healing or otherwise – then it is vital that we make a priority of being filled and re-filled with the empowering presence of the Holy Spirit. The Bible shows us that this is not a one-off experience for followers of Christ, but an ongoing need. The disciples in the early Jerusalem church who were filled with the Spirit at Pentecost (Acts 2:4) were filled again a few days later, after they had prayed for Peter and John's release from prison (Acts 4:31). Paul was not only filled with the Spirit when Ananias prayed for him (Acts 9:17), but also when he was ministering in Paphos (Acts 13:9). The Bible urges us to be filled and to keep being filled, so we need to pray and seek this regularly. It may help you to ask someone who is obviously ministering in the power of the Spirit to pray for you for a similar filling. If you believe God is clearly calling you to be involved in healing ministry, then ask someone already ministering healing to pray for you to receive an impartation of the Spirit's power in this area. Although we can, and should, pray for ourselves for this, it seems that God especially honours those who are humble enough to ask others to pray for them in this way.

From time to time I deliberately go to healing meetings where I know someone with a mature ministry of healing is speaking, both with a desire to learn more from what I

see and hear, and with a desire for some further impartation of God's Spirit for this ministry. A few years ago
Anne and I were at a series of such meetings led by someone whose style is somewhat different from ours, but who
was being greatly used by God in healing. We, together
with many others, asked this person to pray for us for a
fresh anointing for this ministry, and we left greatly
encouraged in faith for God to use us. On our return to
our church we advertised a special meeting for anyone
interested to hear about our trip, and to come asking God
for healing. Patrick was suffering from a blood disorder,
two hernias and sclerosis of the liver. He had been getting
progressively worse over a number of months, even
though some in our church had been praying for him regularly. He had got to the stage of spending over twenty
hours a day in bed, and the doctors were saying they
could not operate because of his blood condition. He was
deteriorating further and was fearful that he was dying.
During the meeting there was a word of knowledge for
someone with a liver condition and I found myself saying
aloud, 'I think that's for you, Patrick.' I had spotted him
looking pale and ill and was so pleased that he had been
able to come to the meeting. He gingerly made his way to
the front for the time of ministry and I and others on the
ministry team prayed for him. From that day on he made
a remarkable and speedy recovery as all his debilitating
symptoms left, until he was completely well again.
Patrick has not suffered from any of those conditions
since, much to the astonishment of his doctors!

Avoiding Abuse

Whenever we are involved with charismatic gifts and
the power of God, it is easy to become focused on them

as if they are the only things that are important in our Christian lives. This can be dangerous if it means we cease to cooperate with God as He seeks to mould our character to become more like Jesus. Although there are contemporary examples of believers being used to heal others while they are not living very holy lives themselves, this is something we must avoid, seeking to exercise our gifts from pure, godly motives. This is the only way in which God can use us on a long term basis.

Jesus faced a test designed to ensure that He would not abuse His power. Immediately following His baptism He was led by the Spirit into the desert where He was tempted by the devil (Luke 4:1–13). Changing stones into bread might have satisfied His immediate physical hunger, and leaping from the temple might have been a spectacular demonstration of power, but both would have involved an abuse of His power. Instead, Jesus rejected the temptation to use His power outside the will of God.

Similarly, the disciples were tempted to abuse the power given to them. Peter was offered money for his gift (Acts 8:18) and James and John wanted to call down fire on Samaritan villages (Luke 9:54). Sadly, recent Christian history reveals that not all believers empowered by the Spirit have resisted such temptations and some have misused the power or authority entrusted to them. Whenever Christians abuse these things, the work of God is brought into disrepute in the eyes of both the Church and the watching world. So as God entrusts to us an understanding of authority and an experience of His empowering, we must be careful not to abuse it.

> 'From everyone who has been given much, much will be demanded; and from the one who has been entrusted with much, much more will be asked.' (Luke 12:48)

I express one note of caution: although we may be out-
raged by God using people who don't appear to be living as holy a life as we would like them to, we can never
overrule or second guess His grace. If we can see the
bigger picture we will understand that God is concerned
for all people all of the time. He is sickened by the preva-
lence of sickness and He wants to see people healed. To
that end, He is often more willing to use people than we
are; this is as true in the area of healing as in any other
way of extending His grace to people in need. Many of
us know people whom God has used to inspire us, or
even lead us to Christ in the first place, whose lives then,
or subsequently, were not adequately sanctified. And
sadly some of those who both follow Jesus and lead
others to Him fall away from faith subsequently. Yet that
doesn't negate the way in which God used them to help
us on the road of faith, nor the validity of what they
taught us along the way. Instead of condemning either
them or the ministry they were involved in, we need to
pray for them for restoration, and for their ministry for
true authenticity. If you know, or know of, someone like
this, take a moment to pray for them that faith and holiness will be re-awakened in them. One of the hardest
fruit of the Spirit to bear consistently is patience – and
especially patience with Christians who, from our point
of view, 'should know better than that!'

One application of this principle is in the way we recruit
people onto healing prayer teams. We need to be careful
that we don't set the holiness bar either too high, thereby
meaning no one is qualified, or too low, thereby bringing
this ministry into disrepute. I remember one woman in
our church coming to me in tears saying that she didn't
think she could ever be good enough to be on the ministry
team. The bar had obviously at that stage been set so high
that it had put her off ever starting to learn.

It is also important to remember that the gifts of the Spirit are not given as rewards for holiness. We see that Paul's letters to the Corinthians were written to a church that experienced a lot of immorality amongst its ranks, and yet, made significant use of the spiritual gifts. Paul's admonition was written to ensure the gifts were used correctly, but he never once suggested that they should stop being used. Instead he encouraged the believers to make sure they were utterly committed to expressing love alongside and as a backdrop to the gifts God had given them.

We need to take a similar approach: we cooperate with God as He seeks to shape and transform our character and we work to use the gifts He has given us with pure motives, out of a desire to see others made whole.

4

Barriers to Involvement

If we accept the premise this book has set out so far, that healing ministry is something that every Christian is meant to exercise, we must ask the question: 'Why aren't more people involved in this ministry today?'

There are several factors which may mean Christians are not involved – either by choice or due to some barrier which is preventing them. Different people will identify with some or all of the factors that I explore below. Each of them, however, can and should be overcome so that we are free to minister just as Jesus did.

Inadequate Worldview

A worldview is very much like a pair of glasses. Everything we see, our perceptions and understanding of the world around us, is filtered and processed by our particular worldview. It shapes the way in which we 'interpret' the world and is such an integral and natural part of us that we are unaware of its influence most of the time.

The problem for Christians living in the West, that is a barrier to us embracing the supernatural, is that we have adopted a worldview at odds with that of the Bible. The worldview of the West in the second part of the 20th century was based on scientific rationalism – unless things could be explained logically or scientifically, it was assumed they could be not trusted as 'true'. This meant there was great scepticism about the existence of God, about the supernatural in general, and the possibility of miracles in particular. In time this worldview has been replaced by post-modernity. This worldview allows for a more personal appropriation of truth. Postmodernism has been defined as 'a worldview characterized by the belief that truth doesn't exist in any objective sense, but is created rather than discovered.' In other words, all truth in the journey of life is relative to the experience of the 'traveller'. Whether we like to think it or not, such worldviews are so ingrained in our Western culture that many believers have unwittingly adopted similar views.

The Bible has a different worldview. The true Christian worldview is not rooted in scientific rationalism or post-modernity, though some elements of both these views may well be true. The Bible reveals a God who is both beyond reason and yet is reasonable. He is able to act in supernatural ways which are true to His character but beyond man's full comprehension. The biblical worldview introduces us to a God who heals – a God who desires to intervene on behalf of His creation when they are in need.

Throughout the Bible many names are attributed to God by which we can understand more of His character and nature. These are names by which God reveals Himself to us and by which He has bound Himself to be faithful. One of these is *Jehovah Rophe*, meaning, '*I am the* LORD, *who heals you*' (Ex. 15:26).

The ways in which God brings healing are various:

- Through the natural healing properties He implanted in the human body when He created it. E.g. a cut finger will be healed 'all by itself' over a period of time if the cut is not infected.
- Through doctors. Medicine and prayer are not at odds with each other. The Bible takes a very positive attitude to the medical practices of its day and modern Christians should have a similar attitude. The medical profession's skill and wisdom in diagnosis and the discovery and prescribing of drugs are God-given – even if they are not always acknowledged to be so.
- Through the use of spiritual gifts (one of which is healings).
- Through prayer and faith.

During one of our 'healing on the streets' prayer sessions a married couple approached and asked our team if we would pray for the man's father, who wasn't present, because he had stomach cancer. We prayed for his father and the couple left. Some months later this same couple returned, this time bringing a friend with them and also her grandmother who had stomach cancer. The man said, 'You prayed for my dad and he was healed. Please will you pray for this lady too?' Although I can't verify this story or the man's healing, it seems as though God touched the man's father as we prayed. Was it the prayer that healed him or the medical treatment he was undergoing? Or was it both? In the minds of this couple, prayer had played a very significant part.

Two of the means of healing listed above are open to reason and science, but the other two are trans-rational. God is sovereign and He is the One who brings healing

through whatever means He chooses. We must, therefore, have a truly biblical worldview that allows for the
supernatural as well as the natural.

Sub-biblical Theology

There are two particular traps that many 'trained theologians' have frequently fallen into in the Western
world, the first of which is adopting a liberal theological
position based on scientific rationalism. The starting
point of such a view is that, rationally speaking, 'miracles cannot occur', so it therefore needs to find ways of
reinterpreting the miracle stories of the Bible and put
forward 'rational' explanations. This erroneous worldview does not take Scripture seriously and seeks to
undermine its authority.

The second type of what I call 'sub-biblical theology'
is the cessationist view. This is the view that the gifts of
the Spirit (and especially the supernatural gifts such as
tongues, healings, miracles etc) were God's gifts for the
early Church only. Cessationists believe that after the
Church was established and the Canon of Scripture was
complete, these gifts ceased to be a part of normal
church life. This view is founded on the belief that those
gifts and that ministry were needed at that stage of the
Church's life to authenticate the truth of what was being
preached. According to this view, even after the Canon
of Scripture was complete, the stories of the miracles in
the gospels were the only ones necessary to demonstrate
Jesus is Saviour and Lord. In other words, we no longer
need miracles to demonstrate the reality of the kingdom
of God.

Though at one stage very popular in the Western
world, this view has a number of keys flaws. Firstly,

it seems to be a theological justification for the experience of a miracle-less Church dominated by a faulty worldview. The answer to a faulty worldview is not to rewrite theology, but to change the presuppositions on which the worldview is based. Start to believe in the possibil-ity of the miraculous and very quickly you will begin to see the miraculous happening!

Secondly, there is no indication in Scripture that the gifts were given for a limited time only or that they would ever cease to be part of church life. In fact, 1 Corinthians 12 implies that they will be here until the time of perfection when Jesus returns. Nowhere in the Bible is there the sense that the gifts are seen to be related to the Canon of Scripture being completed.

Thirdly, in the light of the phenomenal growth of the Pentecostal and Charismatic Church worldwide during recent decades, such a view is credible only if the experience of the miraculous of countless millions of Christians is discounted as self-delusion or being of demonic origin. If it is true that, *'By their fruit you will recognise them* [false prophets]' (Matt. 7:16), then the evidence of lives changed, people saved, healed and delivered, and the works of love and mercy bringing relief and help to the poor seem to suggest the authenticity of these people's faith and that these gifts come from our living God.

For a long time I had an inadequate theology concerning the things of the Spirit. I pretty much disregarded the gifts of the Spirit as being irrelevant to modern believers. For that reason I had no sense at all that healing was available to the Church today. During my church upbringing these things were not taught, not practised, and if they were mentioned they were referred to from the dispensational cessationist viewpoint expressed above.

I remember that while I was training for ordination and on holiday at home in Leeds, the *Yorkshire Evening Post* ran a full centre-spread feature on David Watson and the miraculous things that were happening in his church in York. My mother, who came from a trad-itional Anglican background, asked me what I thought about all this talk of speaking in tongues and praying for healing. She was genuinely interested in the possi-bility of God so caring for the broken that He would empower His Church to minister healing. At the same time she was probably somewhat anxious about such a strange phenomenon as 'speaking in tongues'. To my rational cessationist mind both were equally off-put-ting, because they were beyond reason, and I recall telling her I thought that such things were marginal to mainstream Christianity in the 20th century. Today, of course, I would assert that they are absolutely central! Interestingly, my mother is not dissimilar from many with a similar liberal western background who have become more open to biblical-based Christianity as a result of experiencing the grace of God as someone has prayed for healing for them.

Looking back I am somewhat horrified by my arro-gance – arrogance in the sense that I thought these things could not be very important if I wasn't involved in them! But I was speaking out of sheer ignorance and I believe that many others approach the subject of heal-ing from a similar place of ignorance, without having had any real exposure to the supernatural power of God. I was certainly not an untypical conservative evangeli-cal, but God in His mercy decided to re-educate me as only He can.

Fear

Apart from reasons to do with our worldview or theology, there are at least two unhealthy barriers which
prevent Christians from participating in healing ministry. The first of these is *fear*. Fear is one of the main
seeds that the enemy sows into the lives of Christians to
make them ineffective in serving God. Fear to do with
the healing ministry can grip us in a number of ways:

- 'What would happen if I prayed for someone to be
  healed and they weren't?' is a common question. We
  have to accept that our Christian lives operate on the
  basis of faith and we need to be prepared to step out
  of the boat and obey the prompting of the Spirit
  when He speaks. As we do that, we are to leave the
  consequences to God. If we are obeying Him then He
  is able to minister His love to people even if they
  aren't immediately healed.

- Similar to this first aspect is the fear of boldly proclaiming the message that 'Our God heals' only to
  find that people who we fully *expected* to be healed are
  not. It raises the question, 'Won't I damage their faith
  and also God's reputation?' I have discovered now,
  having prayed for hundreds of people, that provided
  we don't promise *immediate healing* when we pray for
  people and that we talk to them about God being their
  Healer, most people won't feel let down. They will be
  blessed that someone cared enough to pray for them.
  Also, God is better at looking after His reputation
  than we are. If we are bold enough to call Him 'the
  God who heals', which is one of the great names by
  which He has revealed himself (Exod: 15.26), then He
  is able to demonstrate the truth of this name.

- Lastly, the fear of many pastors is, 'What will happen if my church starts praying for the sick? I won't be able to cope with the pastoral difficulties this will raise if people aren't healed!' Such fears cause many ministers to back off from releasing their people into this ministry. But the answer to abuse of any ministry is not *non-use*, but *correct* use. When I first wanted to introduce this ministry in our church on Sundays I had to face this fear in myself. I did so first by doing some systematic teaching on the subject in Sunday sermons. At the same time, I trained a ministry team and then publicly authorised them for this ministry, in the belief that this would also allay the fears of some in the congregation that I was just letting everyone 'have a go' (I was actually letting this happen in the home groups, but I felt a different approach was necessary for Sunday services). I made this team directly accountable to me and met with them frequently to discuss progress and difficulties, and so that we could share the wonderful stories of what God was doing. I was trying to ensure that we were doing things as in the New Testament Church, 'decently and in order'. Sometimes people have joined the church who have been trained to minister healing in a different way based on a different model. I normally ask those people to be willing to adopt our model for this ministry while they are in meetings associated with our church. In this way I try to create a spiritual climate for which I am happily answerable to God for the way in which prayer ministry is done, and where both my fear and the fear of others about inappropriate ways of ministering healing are minimised.

I understand from experience that church leaders are particularly vulnerable to fear in this area. When you are running a church you feel the need to be able to explain to people what is going on, after all, you are paid to know what's going on! But ultimately God is the only One in charge and leaders have to accept that much of healing ministry is trans-rational – we will never be able to explain or understand it fully. Allied to this is the fear that if we launch such a ministry we won't be able to control it – and not necessarily in a wrong sense, but out of our desire to protect the church congregation. Again, we have to accept that there will always be things that are out of our control, even though it makes us feel uncomfortable. In many ways, the less we are in control and the more God is the better!

Ultimately, these and other fears are based on lies of the enemy, who would like us to believe that if we relinquish control and trust God everything will go wrong. Faith overcomes fear. We can be free from such anxieties by applying biblical truth and putting our trust in God.

Apathy

The second unhealthy barrier, after fear, is that of apathy. Sometimes non-believers appear to have more sympathy than Christians when people are sick! They will normally say something like, 'I hope you get well soon.' This seems to be a God-given reaction which remains within people despite the fall. They say it out of concern and compassion. For some reason, some Christians almost seem to have less sympathy for the sick, not being sure whether God will heal them or whether he wants to 'teach them through suffering'. This longing for healing that is present in non-believers ought to be present in even greater measure, with greater understanding and with greater hope in those who are now 'in Christ'.

The life of the Spirit ought to be flowing out through us as it did through Jesus, and when we see someone who is sick our reaction ought to be the same as His:

> 'When Jesus landed and saw a large crowd, he had **compassion** on them and healed their sick.' (Matt. 14:14)

Perhaps some of us have lost the compassion that Jesus had? Maybe we have become apathetic to the pain and need of the broken lives of people all around us? Perhaps sometimes we even justify our apathy by talking about the priority of evangelism so that we might 'save their souls' instead? Whatever the reason, when we surrender to God and truly seek Him to transform us, as the Spirit of God comes upon us in power He always renews our compassion for people.

This is one of the first things God did for me when He touched me by the power of His Spirit. I found a new empathy with people so that I would be deeply moved whenever I saw someone who was sick and in need of healing. Since then I have seen it time and again as we have prayed for others to be filled afresh. Those who were previously trapped in apathy and indifference have their hearts warmed and demonstrate it by beginning to reach out to those in need. The Holy Spirit is the Spirit of compassion and He makes us much more sensitive to the needs of others. I have known people find themselves weeping as they watch the evening news because of a heightened awareness of people's pain. Repetitive exposure to stories of murder and poverty on the news do desensitise us, but the Spirit reawakens our godly compassion.

When we are faced with those in need, it is a natural godly reaction to want to do something about it. For myself, I have experienced this often as a 'physical' feeling of longing to see wholeness come. This tangible longing is something like that which Jesus displayed in His ministry. When we read in our Bibles that He had 'compassion', the original Greek is the word *splagchni-zomai*, which conveys the meaning of feeling something in one's 'guts'. True compassion is not a cerebral thing, but a visceral thing.

Compassion can be costly. It is easy to say a few comforting words to someone. Words don't cost us very much. It is much more costly to take the time to pray for them and minister to them. When we begin to pray and ask God's Spirit to come we are involved in such a way that we *must* hear from God and pray appropriately. But we need to be prepared to do it and overcome our apathy, even if we are already tired and exhausted.

I remember on one occasion I was exhausted at the end of a Sunday morning service and having said goodbye to most people, I became aware that someone was 'hovering' waiting to have a word with me. I was looking forward to lunch, but somehow summoned up the energy to ask what the issue was that concerned him. He told me his daughter who was a gym teacher had been off work for a number of weeks with a leg injury that wasn't getting better and he was really concerned for her and wanting me to pray with him for her healing. There was something in the way he said it that caught my attention; something welled up in me longing for her to be healed, and I sensed that he had faith for her healing there and then. Tired as I was, I prayed with him, asking Jesus to come by His Spirit to his daughter and bring healing. I found myself speaking to her leg and commanded healing as if she were present. That evening, much to my surprise, this man greeted me as I arrived for our informal service which he didn't normally attend. He had a big smile on his face and told me how his daughter had rung him up and told him that in the middle of the afternoon she had felt as if warm oil was being massaged into her calf resulting in all her pain leaving and full, pain free mobility being restored. 'Have you been praying for me today, Dad?' was her question. 'You can be sure of that' was his reply 'and praise God, He has answered our prayers.' He had come to church that night to thank God publicly for his daughter's healing. *'I will declare your name to my brothers; in the congregation I will praise you'* (Ps. 22:22).

It has to be a conscious choice we make to minister the love of God to others. God will honour this and time and again will act supernaturally on our behalf.

Inappropriate Model

For many years there were three dominant models available to the Church which moulded the way in which healing ministry was exercised in most churches. God has wonderfully used many of those who pioneered or adopted one or another of these different approaches and through them brought healing to many. But at the same time, God is still wanting a vast army of His servants equipped to serve Him in this way.

The healing models in use can be broadly categorised as follows:

• The sacramental model dominates the traditional churches. It is dependant on a properly trained and appointed leadership who exercise this ministry in a highly controlled environment and normally with a certain amount of accompanying religious practise and ritual. Healing might be administered at the communion rail alongside communion and with the use of liturgical prayer and sometimes a liturgical response. While this has been effective for some, it limits the numbers of those who can minister healing to those who are suitably 'qualified', and it limits the beneficiaries to those willing to go through the required spiritual hoops of church attendance and ritual.

- The Eldership model is based on the instructions in the book of James (James 5:13–16). Any member of the church who is sick, and whose own prayers for their recovery seem to be going unanswered, is invited to call for the elders of the church to come and pray for them. Sometimes anointing with oil accompanies the prayer. This model has the benefit of taking the healing ministry into the homes of believers, but sadly tends to keep the ministry in the hands of a small number of church members (only the elders), restricts healing to believers, and because it happens in homes rather than public church meetings, results in very little visibility for this ministry. The consequence is that in many churches it is rarely used except as a 'last resort'.

- The Pentecostal model dominates the Pentecostal and new churches. It is usually dependant on an anointed man or woman of God exercising this ministry, often in a highly charged emotional environment with a great emphasis on faith – almost expressing faith in faith itself. This ministry may be very effective, but it also seems to depend on 'superstars' and doesn't naturally and obviously result in releasing this ministry to ordinary Christians in the way that Jesus envisaged. Moreover, it seems to imply faith and emotion must go hand in hand, whereas in the New Testament faith is exhibited in different ways by different people.

John Wimber introduced many of us to another model and this **integrated model** is the basis for ministering healing which New Wine has adopted and has used to train people for more than fifteen years. We will turn our attention to this model in detail in the next chapter. Suffice to say for now that it is based on trying to minister healing in the same non-religious way that Jesus healed people – in a way that is equally applicable in church services, in homes, in workplaces, or in public on the street, and which any Christian, rather than just a select few can learn.

If you know that any of these, or other issues, have stopped you from committing yourself to being involved in healing ministry, despite feeling a calling to do so, you can be set free as you acknowledge the nature of the trap, repent and pray for release and freedom. It may help you to ask others to pray over you in a similar vein.

Does God Really Want to Heal Me?

As we conclude this chapter, let's think briefly about a different kind of barrier – the barrier that prevents people from asking for prayer in the first place. Many people share a common struggle when it comes to prayer for healing: 'Does God actually want to heal *me*?' To answer this question we can turn to Matthew 8, which documents the first detailed story of an individual who was healed by Jesus.

Jesus and His disciples had been travelling around preaching the good news (Matt. 4); then Jesus set out His core teaching on the sermon on the mount (Matt. chs 5 – 7). From chapter 8 onwards in Matthew's Gospel we see an expansion and demonstration of what Jesus had been proclaiming with a series of healings. Matthew 8 lists four specific incidents – a man with leprosy, a Centurion's servant, Peter's mother-in-law and a demon-possessed man – and tells us that, '. . . *many who were demon-possessed were brought to him, and he drove out the spirits with a word and healed all the sick'* (Matt. 8:16).

The man with leprosy approached Jesus with some caution, unsure as to how He would react.

> 'A man with leprosy came and knelt before him and said, "Lord, if you are willing, you can make me clean."' (Matt. 8:2)

It seems as if he was uncertain about whether Jesus was really willing to heal him. This is exactly the same uncertainty as those who think, 'Lord, are you really willing to heal *me*?' Have you noticed that many Christians have this uncertainty not just for themselves, but also for others as they pray? They often offer God a get-out clause by adding a caveat, so their prayer becomes, 'I pray that this will happen . . . *God willing.*' It seems as if this uncertainty is endemic whether we live in the first or twenty-first century.

So we need to take special notice and assurance from the fact that this issue of willingness is the very first issue Jesus addresses. He says to the man, '*I am willing!*' He says the same to us today. The willingness of God to bring healing ought not to be a question for us. Jesus answered it unequivocally. God is absolutely committed to our wholeness – that can never be in doubt. Healing is never a question of *whether God will give healing,* it is only ever a question of *when* God will give healing. The glorious Christian truth about healing is that if we are not healed while we are in our mortal bodies we will be completely healed when we are given our new, immortal bodies when we pass from this life to the next. There is no doubt that having a proper expectation of the return of Jesus and His final victory when 'all things are made new' will give us a greater faith in God's power to heal today, and also a greater peace in waiting for healing that seems a long time coming. If it doesn't happen here on Earth, Heaven is the ultimate place of our complete healing.

Part 2

Releasing the Ministry

5

An Integrated Healing Model

In the previous chapter we saw that various models are used by the Church to facilitate healing ministry, but that they tend to take on the characteristics of their own denomination or stream, making them accessible to limited groups of people. What I long to see is a model for healing being practiced that is open to all, can be used by ordinary Christians, and travels beyond the walls of our churches to where it is really needed: on the streets and in the homes and workplaces of the needy who don't yet know Christ. I hope the model offered in this chapter goes some way to achieving that.

There are two elements basic to this model. First is the example of Jesus Himself, and second is the need to find a model that is appropriate in almost any context and is possible for every Christian to follow. It's when the natural and supernatural combine, as they did in Jesus, that this ministry will gain its greatest credibility and reach the most people.

At the heart of this model is a moment-by-moment dependence on the Holy Spirit. Healing ministry is about co-operating with God and what He is doing in a person's life as they come to Him. It is vital then that we regularly feed and nurture our own relationship with God. We first need to be in a place where we can clearly hear His Holy Spirit if we are to be able to be prompted by Him while we are ministering and also grow in our effectiveness in ministry.

General Principles

First, here are some general principles to bear in mind as you prepare to pray for someone.

- Pay attention both to your spiritual relationship with the Lord, to your behaviour and attitudes, your personal hygiene, and anything else which might adversely affect your physical relationship to the person being prayed for.
- Wherever possible, pray in pairs, including someone of the same sex as the sick person. Jesus sent the disciples out in pairs and we do well to follow this example – it helps both discernment and faith.
- When you begin a prayer session, ask the person what they want Jesus to do for them. We are helping them to reach out to receive healing from Him. In doing this we are trying to get their attention off us and onto the Lord – He is the only One who can heal anyone.
- Explain how you will pray – this is especially important when praying for people who have had no previous experience of being ministered to for healing. Although you may be nervous, they will be even more so. A little explanation can help allay their fears.
- Pray with your eyes open while encouraging the sick person to have their eyes closed. This will enable you to see whether the person is 'at ease' while being

prayed for, and also to see what God is doing while you are praying. (It can be hard to learn to pray with eyes open for those used to prayer meetings where bowed heads and shut eyes are the norm! But imagine Jesus on the road stopping to pray for the sick – when He touched their eyes or ears surely He would have had His eyes open.)

- Lay hands carefully on the person in an appropriate way. Normally this should be gently on the shoulder or forehead as well as on the painful part of their body, provided that is appropriate. In some cases it is more appropriate to ask the person being prayed for to place their own hand on the painful part of their body, if it is in a 'sensitive' area.

- Never exert pressure on a person as if to push them over. Sometimes a person may fall under the power of this encounter with God, as happened to Abraham (Gen. 17:3), Moses (Num. 20:6), Daniel (Dan. 10:9), John (Rev. 1:17) and others. If this does happen, break the person's fall if possible and let them down gently. (Another good reason for keeping our eyes open is to see when this is happening so we can take appropriate action, helping them to fall without harming themselves.)

- Sometimes a person being prayed for may experience acute pain or feel particularly hot or cold. These may indicate that God is 'doing something'. If the hot or cold spot is under one of the hands of those praying, move that hand to the painful part of the person being prayed for (again, only do this if appropriate.) These signs are not conclusive evidence that God is healing. Sometimes a lot of heat is experienced and there is no apparent healing, and sometimes nothing is felt and yet healing may occur immediately or follow later.

How people react when the power of God touches them will vary from person to person, but occurrences such as those mentioned above are fairly common. It should not surprise us that people speak of feeling heat pass through their body or of feeling very cold in the part of their body that needs healing, since these things have their parallel in healing without prayer. Eradicating pain with heat is a natural healing process – people apply deep heat or heat pads to relieve back pain etc. Similarly ice packs or ice baths are used by sportspeople to deal with swelling and aid muscle repair.

Sometimes a person will say, as you begin to pray for them, that the pain you are praying for has moved to a different part of their body. This can be an indication that the source of the sickness is demonic in origin – as though the root of the pain is trying to evade our attention. If you notice something like this and sense the Holy Spirit confirming that the cause is demonic, you may need to pray specifically for deliverance. This is a type of prayer that warrants a specific approach and you can find out more about it in chapter 12.

Other physical signs that the Holy Spirit is touching a person may include them feeling shaky or light-headed after prayer – as though they are coming round after an anaesthetic. Others will say they feel an incredible sense of peace. To me, this is a very important, authenticating mark of healing prayer – an abiding sense of God's peace. We notice that when Jesus appeared to His disciples in the upper room after His resurrection, He breathed on them and said, 'My peace be with you' (John 20). God's peace is an indication of His presence.

My wife, Anne and I, once prayed for a lady who was very anxious because she and her husband had decided to move away from our area. She had only recently become a Christian and her marriage didn't feel very secure at that time, since her husband showed no interest in her faith. They had decided to move from London and she was worried about finding a new church and making new friends. After praying for her for a while, we asked how she was feeling and she said, 'I feel such peace.' Then she said, 'I could get addicted to this!' It was so satisfying for her to feel the peace and wellbeing God had instilled in her that she didn't want it to leave. At the end of our prayer session she left a different person, feeling able to face all that was ahead. Such peace should accompany our ministry to others. If a person does not feel at peace at the end, it probably means there is a need for further prayer.

A Model For Ministry

What follows is not meant to be a rigid formula, but is intended as a guideline. It is based around five questions. We are principally asking these questions of God, although we can also address some of them to the person we are ministering to. We are expecting revelation from God, as well as information from the sick person. These five stages of the ministry model are . . .

- The interview – What is the problem?
- The diagnosis – Where does it come from?
- Prayer selection – How shall I pray?
- Taking stock – What is happening?
- Post-prayer advice – Where do we go from here?

1. The interview – what's the problem?

We begin by asking the sick person what ministry is wanted. Jesus sometimes asked this even when the answer seemed obvious. When He ministered to two blind men He asked them, *'What do you want me to do for you?'* (Matt. 20:32). The men replied, *'Lord ... we want our sight.'* Then we read that, *'Jesus had compassion on them and touched their eyes. Immediately they received their sight and followed him'* (Matt. 20:34).

Follow up this initial question with further questions as necessary, such as,

'How long have you had this problem?'

'Has it been diagnosed by a doctor?'

'Are you taking medication?'

A long medical explanation from the sick person is not necessary, since we are not doctors, nor are we trying to replace the medical profession in that sense. But as the person begins to answer we should be silently praying and asking the Lord, 'What is the root of this problem?'

2. The diagnosis – where does it come from?

People may be sick for a variety of reasons. The root of the sickness could be:

- A purely physical sickness
- Association with some trauma
- Psychosomatically induced
- A result of sin (e.g. sexually transmitted diseases)
- A generational sickness within the family
- A consequence of a demonic oppression
- The result of a curse

The person may give us some clue as to the root cause of the problem if we ask some further, sensitively phrased questions as the Spirit prompts. For example, 'Were your symptoms preceded by any emotional shock or trauma (e.g. a death, a divorce, a separation, the loss of a job, etc)?'

At the same time we should be praying silently for discernment in case the real problem is unrepented sin or suppressed shock or grief etc. We may not get any direct clue immediately from either the Lord or the sick person, but we can still continue as the answer to this question may become clear as we progress. We must be careful not to insist we are right in our perception and if we sense it is the result of some sin we must never be accusatory or condemning. It is better simply to encourage some 'heart searching' and tell the person that they should seek forgiveness 'for anything the Lord reveals to you.'

In many cases, sickness is the result of some long held traumatic experience. People often suffer trauma in their lives which they carry around silently and no one knows the extent to which it has scarred their consciousness and affects their behaviour. It is not uncommon for people to 'hold on' to such issues for many years before they are ever dealt with. For this reason we need to create a 'safe environment' whenever we minister, so that people feel at ease and can begin to allow these things to come to the surface. I often use the illustration of our lives being like soil with stones hidden beneath the surface. The stones are hidden from sight, but when it rains consistently on the ground, they are brought up and exposed. At that point it is easy to pick the stones out and dispose of them. This is what happens when the Holy Spirit comes. His presence is like the rain, gently washing through us, so that the hidden blockages that cause us problems are brought to the surface where they can be easily dealt with and removed.

3. Prayer selection – how shall I pray?

Our normal starting point is to invite the Holy Spirit to come with His power to heal. Then we wait, while praying silently in tongues if that gift has been released in you. (The use of tongues in healing is significant. First, it helps to tune in to the Lord, and what He is saying or doing; second, as we pray in tongues the Spirit Himself is praying through us in a focused and relevant way, even when we don't know precisely how to pray.) It's better to intercede *silently* in tongues because praying aloud in tongues can be very off-putting to the sick person. We want them to concentrate on Jesus, not our prayers. We should not be surprised if, at this point, the enemy comes to put us out of action with temptations which make us feel ashamed or with feelings of uselessness which make us feel unworthy and not up to the task. For instance, I have discovered that when praying in a team with others for a young woman, young men have suddenly been assaulted by unclean sexual thoughts about her. This is typical of the enemy's tactics and reveals his consistent attempt to stop us praying for each other. What should you do in such circumstances? First, recognise it as the enemy's attack, then resist it, confess it silently to the Lord, ask for fresh compassion and above all persevere in seeking to hear the Lord's voice. There is an old saying about the difference between temptation and sin which is important to remember here: 'You can't stop a bird from flying over your head, but you can stop it building a nest in your hair!'

What is important is to try to 'track' the Holy Spirit during the time of prayer ministry and to pray in other ways as He prompts.

Many of us learn to pray intercessory prayers at an early stage of our Christian life. But when Jesus ministered healing, His prayers were quite different. He often addressed the illness or the person directly as the power of God flowed through Him. So we need to learn how and when to pray as Jesus did. Here are some examples:

- Touch and command healing to the whole person
  *'Jesus reached out his hand and **touched** the man. "I am willing," he said. "Be clean!" And immediately the leprosy left him.'* (Luke 5:13)
- Command to the afflicted part of the body
  'He looked up to heaven and with a deep sigh said to him, "Ephphatha!" (which means, 'Be opened'). At this, the man's ears were opened.' (Mark 7:34)
- Declaration
  *'Hearing this, Jesus said to Jairus, "Don't be afraid; just believe, and **she will be healed**."'* (Luke 8:50)
- Rebuke
  *'So he bent over her and **rebuked** the fever, and it left her. She got up at once and began to wait on them.'* (Luke 4:39)
- Command
  *'Jesus had **commanded** the evil spirit to come out of the man.'* (Luke 8:29)

It will probably seem quite strange initially to speak to a part of a person's body rather than to the person as a whole being. I remember one of our church members finding it very difficult in one of her first times of praying when she was praying for a woman's foot to be healed. The person was lying on the floor (having fallen under the power of Spirit) and our trainee having ascertained the nature of the problem had gently laid her hand on the injured foot. It took her quite some time to pluck up courage to say aloud, 'Foot, be healed, in the name of Jesus'. However, I encourage you not to be afraid of praying in the same way that Jesus did, and to speak directly to the afflicted part of the body when circumstances and the Spirit indicate this is the right thing to do. Incidentally, I always think it best to say these words overtly in the name of Jesus e.g. 'I command this fever in the name of Jesus to be gone.' It makes it clear to everyone, the sufferer, the accompanying friends, and any attendant demons that our faith is in Jesus as the Healer, not in ourselves, or any other occult power.

During this time keep . . .

- . . . acknowledging, blessing, honouring and thanking God for all that He is doing.
- . . . asking God to keep increasing His power to heal.
- . . . being open to the manifestations of the Spirit's power – shaking, weeping, falling etc. If the sick person is unfamiliar with these things, it is good to interpret them e.g. 'That is the power of God – He is at work here.'
- . . . quietly asking the Lord for more revelation to know how to pray more precisely.

4. Taking stock – what's happening?

Francis McNutt has identified four possible effects of our prayers:

- Immediate healing, in which case give thanks and glory to God.
- Partial healing – as with the blind man Jesus healed in Mark 8:

> 'He took the blind man by the hand and led him outside the village. When he had spit on the man's eyes and put his hands on him, Jesus asked, "Do you see anything?" He looked up and said, "I see people; they look like trees walking around." Once more Jesus put his hands on the man's eyes. Then his eyes were opened, his sight was restored, and he saw everything clearly.' (Mark 8:23–5)

We discover whether there has been partial healing by asking at some stage, 'What is happening? Is there any improvement?' If there has been pain when a part of the body is moved, or a loss of mobility, encourage them to gently try the same movement again to see if there has been any change in the symptoms. More ministry might be necessary either on this occasion or at another time. Always give the sick person the option of continuing or stopping the ministry at any stage, and always give them some idea of when they can be prayed for again.

Some people worry that if they ask a question or speak in the middle of this prayer encounter they will 'interrupt' the flow of what God is doing. Be assured that you won't. Once we have asked the Holy Spirit to come, He comes and begins to work. From then on it is fine to ask how He is working and what He is doing. Our aim should always be to find out what the Lord is doing and cooperate with Him. The answer to this question can only come either by revelation through the gifts of the Spirit or by asking the person a question. Just as Jesus asked the blind man, 'Do you see anything?' we can always ask questions without fear of stopping God from working.

Asking questions such as these also means that people will generally tell you when they feel they've had enough prayer or their problem is resolved. Or they may talk about things in such a way that you realise you need to go on and pray further. But we mustn't be afraid of prayer ministry being an open dialogue.

- Delayed healing – as with the leprous men. Here we find an example of people who were healed after they left Jesus, rather than while they were with Him.

> When he saw them, he said, "Go, show yourselves to the
> priests." And as they went, they were cleansed. (Luke
> 17:14)

Sometimes healing is progressive over a period of time.
We may pray for a person once or regularly and frequently, and God heals them over a number of days or
weeks.

When sickness persists, despite continued prayer, an
option to consider is what Francis McNutt calls 'soaking
prayer'. In this approach, a person is prayed over regularly for long periods and encouraged to spend time
soaking in God's presence. This has often brought healing for those with serious, long term conditions.

One lady who attended our church was troubled by a
severe pain in her back which became more acute over
a period of weeks until she was finally diagnosed with a
large cyst and a fibroid on one of her ovaries. She immediately began asking for prayer on almost any and every
possible occasion; she was now being prayed for both by
her house group and the healing ministry team. Her
doctor fixed an appointment at the hospital for a hys-
terectomy, but as a result of the continuous healing
prayer the cyst and fibroid gradually disappeared and
she finally avoided the need for surgery as the Lord
healed her.

- No healing. Sometimes it appears as if nothing has
  happened. We must be careful not to say that a person
  is healed when plainly they are not. Normally, even if
  there is no change in the presenting condition, the Lord
  will have been ministering to the person in some other
  area of their life. Try to discern what this has been, so
  that the person can leave encouraged by God's love
  and grace. At the same time, if the presenting condition

is unchanged, offer another opportunity for prayer on another occasion.

5. Post-prayer advice – where do we go from here?

It is important to know when and how to conclude a time of prayer ministry. We need to be sensitive to the person and their desires, and at the same time to the Lord and what He is doing. Even if it appears that a person is healed, we must not tell them to come off any medication a doctor has prescribed. If they are really healed, their body will begin to react against the medication and it is the doctor's job to lower the dose or stop the treatment completely.

To me, the evidence of healing is healing! If a person is well, then the symptoms of their sickness will have disappeared. If they really are healed, then they will not return for more prayer later. We should not be hasty to conclude that a person is healed until we are sure. Most pain can be massaged to relieve it temporarily, but this doesn't deal with the root cause. When we pray with people, the peace of God will come upon them and during this time their sense of pain may well diminish, but that doesn't mean the root condition has necessarily been cured. If someone appears to be healed and exhibits a loss of symptoms which later return, it usually means that the real cause of the problem has not been dealt with. This might be because the person has not been forthcoming enough during the interview phase or simply because we have not asked the right questions. This is why it is so important for the person praying to exercise discernment. If a person's symptoms do return after prayer, then more prayer is needed. We should also encourage the person to pray effectively for themselves by,

- Remembering what God did previously and thanking Him for the reality of that partial healing.
- Resisting the return of the symptoms – in prayer, refusing to accept back what God has taken away.

If the symptoms continue to re-appear, encourage them to ask others to pray with them once again for the healing to return and remain.

If a person doesn't exhibit any measure of healing:

- It is vital to help them to know that God is still for them and not against them. They might easily feel guilt for not being healed. If there has been an overemphasis on faith they can feel guilty that it is their lack of faith that has kept them unhealed. If this happens, their state is now worse since they are sick spiritually as well as physically!
- Try to leave everyone with an assurance of God's loving presence and the knowledge that He will never abandon them.
- Help them to know that they can go on praying for their healing on their own. This is better and more biblical advice than telling them to 'go and claim your healing' as some tend to do. Healing is a gift from God as a result of His grace and mercy. We need to beware that we don't misread the priorities on God's agenda for each person for whom we pray.
- Offer them the opportunity for more prayer ministry. 'We would love to pray for you again' is an invitation that helps people to know there is no shame in not yet being healed. (This should not be the offer of a private appointment, but of another opportunity in the church's calendar and building.)

Sometimes it is useful to give people some words of Scripture to hold on to, and with which to build their trust in God's goodness. Alternatively, God may have given words of knowledge or prophecy during the prayer ministry which can be held on to and prayerfully applied over the following days. Jean Darnell used to give Scripture verses to people she ministered to as though she was dispensing medicine! They were encouraged to learn these scriptures by heart, taking them deep into their spirits, and meditate on them daily. Sometimes she would see people for a few minutes of prayer on a weekly basis and give them a new verse to learn and embed in their lives each week. We can never underestimate the power of God's Word in the healing process. As the Psalmist wrote, "I *have hidden your word in my heart that I might not sin against you'* (Psalm 119:11).

Whenever possible, after prayer, encourage people to become fully involved in the healing community of the local church if they are not already. The church is meant to be a healing community and so healing can come through any and every aspect of the church's life: through times of public worship, times of fun fellowship, through wholesome relationships either with peers or with those of another generation, and through good teaching as well as through further prayer ministry. Participation in the regular life of the local church is the best way of continuing to grow into the wholeness that Jesus wants His disciples to know, and be known for.

Avoiding Bizarre Methods of Prayer

At all times we are seeking to practice a model of ministry that is accessible to all. In certain situations I have seen methods of prayer used that if an unbeliever saw them they would find weird. Instead we want to minister the grace and power of God to others in such a way that it attracts observers and doesn't make anyone feel uncomfortable.

On one occasion I saw a lady clapping her hands loudly in a circular motion around the torso of the person she was praying for. Another vicar told me of a person who, when praying for someone prostrate on the floor, had their hand on the person's stomach and rubbed it round and around in a circle. We must ask ourselves, 'What is that achieving and how does it look to others?' The likelihood is that it's not necessary at all and is merely an affectation of the person praying. When I see this kind of thing I ask myself whether I would be happy being prayed for in such a way.

I believe we should avoid any method of praying that is visually off-putting. Our aim should be to pray simply like Jesus did – which means being able to pray for people even in public and demonstrating the love and power of God, rather than an 'affected' style of prayer. Someone once coined the phrase 'being naturally supernatural' and this sums up the right approach very well. Although we might think some of Jesus' ways of ministering healing were somewhat bizarre, an awareness of the context will help us see they are not as odd as might first appear. On one occasion he mixed spittle with mud and wiped it on a blind man's eyes. But in His day this was deemed to have medicinal properties, so all that He was doing was fitting in with the accepted medical practice of the day. It didn't appear to them to be 'weird' at all. Healing can and should happen naturally wherever and whenever – we ought to be able to pray for people anywhere without offending either them or onlookers. Over the years I have found myself praying in this way for healing at parties, in shops, on buses, and on the streets, often quietly and in a corner, and seen God touching people in those places with His grace and power. If we pray for someone in a bizarre way it will be distracting for them and make it harder for them to experience God's presence. Our aim should be to pray for them in such a way that it is easy for them to listen to and respond to the Lord, rather than to us as the pray-er.

God Can Heal People Without Our Intervention

We should encourage people to understand that it's not important who prays for them, but *to Whom* we are praying. The person ministering healing is only acting as a catalyst to enable something that God Himself is doing. When we invite people to prayer we are inviting them to come to God and receive from Him, not the ministry team.

It is quite possible for God to touch people and heal them spontaneously without any intervention from us. Some time ago Anne and I attended a conference in Sweden. After the worship at the beginning of the meeting there was a sweet sense of the presence of God and Anne, who was leading the meeting, felt prompted to say, 'That was such a wonderful time of encountering God, I wonder if there is anybody who was healed here?' Immediately a lady at the back of the room raised her hand and said, 'Yes, I think I have been healed.' She said she had come into the meeting suffering from intense stomach pain and now the pain had gone.

We thanked God, not really knowing much about her condition, but the next day we had the opportunity to ask her about it. She was probably in her forties and she told us that she had suffered from almost consistent stomach pain as a result of food allergies from the age of ten years old. We ended up praying with her and her husband and daughter, who were already in the process of coming back to faith as a result of her healing. They were in floods of tears as God's presence came and embraced them with love. Her husband had not been at the meeting the previous day, but had come simply because his wife had been healed. We heard from her 6 months later that she was eating normally, radiant in her faith, and worshipping God along with her restored-to-faith husband and daughter. Her whole family had been healed! If the power of God can touch and heal people even when we are not praying for them, it shouldn't surprise us when they get healed when we *do* pray for them!

6

Sensitivity to the Holy Spirit

The Gifts of the Spirit

We need to understand that this healing ministry is the work of God. *We* cannot heal anyone in our own strength. So we are utterly dependent on the Lord and His direction regarding when and how to pray. To that end, our greatest asset is our sensitivity to the Holy Spirit and our ability to hear Him clearly, so we need to develop our 'hearing' and learn to use the gifts of the Spirit as we minister.

Jesus used many of the gifts of the Spirit when He healed people. In the healing of the paralysed man in Mark 2, for instance, we see several gifts – discernment, knowledge, wisdom, faith and miracles – all coming in quick succession as the Spirit of God prompts and equips Him in this healing encounter. In my under-standing, the first and best place to learn about how the gifts of the Spirit can be used is in the gospels as we see them being used by Jesus. In these stories we see both how Jesus, as a man fulfilled with the Spirit, was dependent on these gifts to bring God's healing, and also how He naturally used these gifts in the course of

His everyday life, mixing and meeting with people in the crowded streets, and in people's homes, as well as in the more obvious (we might suppose) place where the believers of His day met in the synagogue. The premise on which I am trying to live my Christian life is that I am called to become more and more like Jesus; so the natural place to learn about the gifts is in the life of Jesus Himself.

Developing this further, Jesus teaches us to pray for the gifts of the Spirit. In the famous passage about prayer where Jesus teaches us to go on asking, seeking and knocking until we receive and find the door is opened, there is an interesting difference in emphasis between the account in Matthew and the account in Luke. Both recall Jesus saying that God is far more generous in giving to His children when they ask than a loving human father is to his children.

> 'If you, then, though you are evil, know how to give good gifts to your children, how much more will your Father in heaven give **good gifts** to those who ask him!' (Matt 7:11)

> 'If you then, though you are evil, know how to give good gifts to your children, how much more will your Father in heaven give the **Holy Spirit** to those who ask him!' (Luke 11:13)

If we put these two passages together we discover that Jesus is promising that God will give the good gifts of the Holy Spirit to every child of His who asks for them! It seems as if Jesus is anticipating that having seen Him using the gifts of the Spirit to minister God's love, including healing, to people, that His disciples would naturally want God to equip and use them in the same way. Jesus is saying, in effect, 'Yes, of course He will – go ahead and ask Him!'

Instead of learning from the gospels and the example of Jesus many turn instead to the epistles and in particular to Paul's first letter to the Corinthians, where we are specifically told that one of the gifts of the Spirit is 'gifts of healings'. This passage is really about the use of the gifts within the context of the local church meeting. Paul seems to be answering various questions raised by the church, which he begins to answer in chapter 11 verse 18 with the phrase *'when you come together as a church'*. He then outlines a number of the supernatural gifts or 'gracings' of the Spirit with which God wants to equip the Church. Whenever the church meets, God wants to release these gifts among us so that everyone is able to minister the love of God to each other in powerful and life-transforming ways. Since every Christian has the Holy Spirit living within them, each of us has the potential to exercise any of the gifts of the Spirit. As the church meets together, God gives these manifestations of the Holy Spirit through those He wishes to use on that particular occasion.

> 'God gives them to each, just as he determines.' (1 Cor. 12:1)

As people first start to exercise these gifts they may do so in a very undeveloped or hesitant way. So, for instance, Paul talks about only *'knowing or prophesying in part'* (1 Cor. 13:9), and that when a prophesy is given it should be carefully *'weighed'* (1 Cor. 14:29) to see if it is authentically from God. The whole thrust of this passage is that all the gifts of the Spirit should be used in *'a fitting and orderly way'*. So churches have a responsibility to train their members in both the right understanding and right use of these gifts.

Probably over a period of time different members of the church will develop skills in the use of some of these gifts to the extent that they can be thought of as having a recognised 'ministry' in the church and they are appointed by God to longer term roles:

> 'God has appointed . . . workers of miracles, also those having gifts of healing . . .' (1 Cor. 12:28)

It is important to grasp this distinction between 'manifestations' of the Spirit – gifts of the Spirit available to any Christian at any time as the need arises and God provides – and the longer term ministries that will emerge over time under the empowering of the Spirit. It is common for Christians to think of the longer term ministry whenever the subject of healing arises – not realising that in fact any and every believer can be used in this way by God if a particular situation calls for it. The fact is, every single believer can minister just like Jesus did, under the 'gracing' of the Spirit, whenever a specific gift is called for.

This is quite different language to that which many use in contemporary church circles, where great emphasis tends to be placed on 'discovering' our long term personal spiritual gift or gifts and a problem that arises from our understanding of the word 'gift'. We have just one word: 'gift', while the New Testament utilises several, and this limits our understanding. Digging deeper we see that the 1 Corinthians 12 gifts are better described as 'momentary anointings' or 'energisings' than permanent 'gifts'. Part of the Holy Spirit's role in our life is to equip us as necessary to minister God's life-transforming power. So we can think of these gifts as God passing us a particular tool we need to fix a specific problem on a particular occasion.

The normal outworking of this is that not everyone will be used by God in equal measure on a long term basis, but we all can be used by God in healing ministry if we ask Him for the gifts of the Spirit at particular times and occasions. We should therefore be alert and open to the possibility of God using us to intervene in someone's life as He prompts us and then empowers us in that situation.

This makes much more sense to me than the other possibility, which is that only a small number of believers will ever be given gifts of healing. Imagine two different scenarios based on the story of a woman in our church going for a walk in the park. As she walked she saw a middle-aged man who was hobbling slowly along the path in front of her. She drew alongside him and said, 'You look as if you are in pain?' 'Yes,' he replied, 'I have gout and the doctor has told me I must walk everyday and it might go away – but it's very painful.' She has two alternatives. On the view that only a few have 'gifts of healing' and that she is not one of them she would have had to say, 'Hold on a moment, we pray for the sick in our church. I can ring the church office and see whether we can get anyone with the gift of healing to leave work and come and pray for you. Or you could come and wait in the church building until one of them can get there to pray for you?' In a church where most people are out at work all day that might have been a long wait! And anyway, is that how Jesus would have reacted? Instead she breathed a short prayer asking for the Lord's help and, as they continued side by side, asked him, 'Can I pray for you for Jesus to heal you? We do that as Christians and we often see Jesus making people better.' He agreed and she prayed briefly, as she had learnt in church, asking simply for his healing and telling the gout to leave his body so that he could walk pain free. He thanked her and she walked on. The next day she was walking in the park again when she saw the same man seemingly walking somewhat more easily. She approached and when he said that it was, 'a little better' she joyfully exclaimed, 'You see, Jesus is making you better.' He allowed her to pray again when she asked. The next day when she was in the park on her daily constitutional there he was again walking normally and happily. He told her he was 'almost without any pain' and added, 'Your Jesus seems to be healing me!'

This is the way in which the healing ministry really makes sense to me. After all, the only hands Jesus has are our hands; the only eyes and ears He has are our eyes and ears. If I am working in an office somewhere, then I can authentically represent Jesus in that place, not just through what I say and how I behave, but by responding to the Spirit and ministering to others as He directs. If someone we work alongside is sick, we stop and ask ourselves, 'What would Jesus do in this situation?' He would almost certainly offer to pray for that person. As I seek to become more like Him it should become more and more natural for me to do the same. And compassion for the sick on its own is never enough to bring healing; the power and gifts of the Spirit are needed too. It's at these points of need that the gifts can function dynamically. Every believer has the potential to use any and all of them depending on the context and circumstances at the time. The primary place in which we learn about the gifts is in the church, but God intends that we should use them in a much wider arena.

Revelation

I want now to look briefly at some ways in which the grace gifts of the Spirit help us in healing ministry especially and relate some examples. Since healing ministry calls for a high degree of discernment, sensitivity and wisdom, receiving revelation from the Holy Spirit is absolutely vital.

How does revelation work? In addition to the biblical precedents we read of that include dreams, visions, trances, voices, angelic visitations and heavenly raptures, it appears that God's people can discern God's thoughts on a particular matter through their 'spiritual senses'.

We can receive 'revelation' or 'knowledge' from God by,

- feeling things
- hearing things (for example, Samuel and Saul of Tarsus)
- seeing things (i.e. visions in which we may see words, names and pictures, etc)
- knowing things (impartation of divine knowledge)
- speaking things
- smelling or tasting things

These promptings of the Spirit can be 'like the flutter of a butterfly's wings'. They come quickly and are gone almost before we realise they are there. As we become ever more sensitive to the Spirit, we become better attuned to these 'impressions' or whispers of His voice and learn to act on them, but it takes some initial courage. It is very easy to rationalise them away as being 'made up'. It does take faith to verbalise what you believe the Spirit has said, but if you never take the risk then you will never see what God can do with your faith and obedience.

Words of Knowledge

Often in healing prayer sessions people are not as forthcoming as they could be or are guarded about revealing too much for some other reason, and this makes accurate, focused praying difficult. Additionally, many people are unaware of the significance of unresolved traumatic events in their lives and the power that these have to make us emotionally or physically sick later in life. In almost all situations, words of knowledge from the Holy Spirit are invaluable as they cut through our barriers and get to the heart of the problem. As you step out in faith and ask the Lord to speak to you, you will be amazed at the accurate insights He will give you. Following are a number of examples from our church ministry and healing on the streets teams.

Charm bracelet

During a North London church equipping day a number of people were being prayed for and a middle-aged lady came forward who complained of a constant pain in her arm. Although he was not a part of the ministry team, a guy on the sound desk saw this lady go forward and immediately felt the Lord say to him that her ailment had something to do with a charm bracelet she wore on her wrist. He couldn't actually see the bracelet from where he was sitting, so he came from behind the sound desk to where she was being prayed for. Now he could clearly see the bracelet. He joined in with the prayer group and suggested that the lady remove her bracelet because he believed her problem was associated with it. She did so and as soon as she took it off, the pain left her arm and she said, 'I'm healed!'

I'm not sure what relevance the bracelet had to her or whether there was some demonic power involved, but clearly it was associated with some stronghold in her life. As she removed the bracelet in obedience to the word of the Lord, the stronghold was broken and the sickness healed.

Old friends

Our street team was praying for a girl in her thirties who came for prayer on the busy high road through the borough. She said she was very lonely and showed some evidence of suffering from depression. One of the team members felt very definitely to say to her as they prayed, 'God will bring old friends back into your life.' They expressed to her that God didn't want her to be lonely and underlined the fact that He cared about her. As soon as they had finished praying and the girl opened her eyes, she stepped back in surprise as an elderly man who was passing by, stopped right in front of her and said, 'Oh, hello! Do you remember me?' The man turned out to be the father of a girlfriend she had been very close to but had somehow lost touch with. God was bringing His word to pass in a very real and immediate way for her. It had a great impact on her.

A daughter in trouble

Sometimes, without there necessarily being a healing, God will give us a word of knowledge for someone that brings comfort and reassurance. It shows people that He knows all about their situation and longs to intervene in their life.

This was true for an Asian lady who came for prayer on the streets. She had asked for prayer because she had a problem with one of her legs, but as they were praying for her one of the team had a very clear vision of a young woman's face and received the word 'daughter' along with it. Prompted by the Spirit she asked, 'Can you tell me, how is your daughter?' The woman looked amazed and replied, 'I am very worried about her. She is abroad in an unhappy marriage and has been the victim of domestic violence. But how do you know?' 'God showed me her,' the team member replied. They proceeded to pray for the daughter and God touched the mother. Before she left she said, 'Now I know that God has seen her and is with her.'

A difficult pregnancy

A young couple began attending our church after drifting away from God for a while. The young lady was in the early stages of her second pregnancy and not long after joining us she came forward for prayer. She was very anxious because her first pregnancy had been difficult and she had consistently lost weight throughout it instead of gaining weight. The birth had been quite dangerous for her. Even now she looked as if she could have been anorexic. As we prayed for her, Anne received a picture of a small girl standing in front of a hospital bed. In the vision an older woman lay in the bed and a great fear was on the little girl. Anne described the picture and asked the young lady, 'Does this mean anything to you?' She replied that it did. When she was around eleven, she was taken to see her grandmother, who she loved dearly, who was dying in hospital. She was overwhelmed with a feeling of powerlessness – here was a person she loved slipping away and she could do nothing about it – and at that moment fear gripped her completely.

Even as she related this to me and Anne, she was shaking with fear as she relived the moment. We prayed over her as if she were a child again, broke the power of the fear in Jesus' name and asked Him to come to her and comfort her. From that day on she went on to carry her baby without difficulty, putting some weight on. Since then she has given birth to two more children without any problems. The fear of losing someone precious to her again had been broken as God set her free from the trauma of the past.

Dreams

Just as He has done with various characters in the Bible, God will often use dreams to impart revelation to us. No distinction regarding their purpose is made in Scripture between words of knowledge and dreams, but perhaps words of knowledge can be understood to be briefer and more immediate, while God uses dreams to speak to us about bigger matters. Whatever their precise purpose, God still uses dreams today when He wants to get our attention and speak to us about something. Just over three years ago He did just this, when He gave Anne an important dream.

We woke up one morning and Anne told me she'd had a strange dream. In it, we were both escaping from our house which was being flooded – so much so that we had scrambled out onto the roof to avoid the rising water. I had used a rope to tie a plank around our chimney and we were attempting to float on it, but the entire house was being submerged and we were still sinking! Though it sounds surreal to put this down in writing now, nevertheless the sense of urgency and panic were very real for Anne at the time. In her dream, as we were floundering in the flood water, she heard the Lord speak to her saying, 'Anne, do you believe in prayer?' She replied, 'Yes Lord!'. Then she woke up.

Anne was left with a very distinct impression after the dream – not that the house was going to be flooded and we'd require the services of a plumber! – but that there was going to be a crisis, during which she would be called upon to pray like she had never prayed before. Though she had no sense of what it might be, she knew that God was preparing her for something.

At 3 o' clock that same day I had a heart attack. I was in our home with one of our daughters when I began to experiencing terrible chest pains. I didn't realise what was happening, but my daughter could see I was in dire straights and called an ambulance. Anne received the phone call telling her to come home immediately and she arrived to find the ambulance crew already there. As the paramedics were helping me to move from the sitting room towards the front door, I collapsed and went into cardiac arrest right in front of Anne. As she knelt beside me, she knew: this was the moment the Lord had warned her about. She began praying more fervently than she had ever done before and the Holy Spirit prompted her to speak Psalm 23 into my ear as the paramedics rushed to fetch the defibrillator from the ambulance and tried to shock my heart back to life.

My heart began beating again – thankfully! The paramedic who used the defibrillator looked just as relieved as Anne, as she explained that not only was this the first time she'd ever had to use them, but also that they only work in approximately one third of cases!

Trusting God

Whether it is using words of knowledge or dreams, frequently we are required simply to trust what God says to us and then pray as He directs. Acting on revelation can seem fraught with risk and make us feel vulnerable, but when we are walking closely with God and have gained some experience of listening to His voice, often these promptings and impressions open the way for Him to act supernaturally in and through us. Very often the significance of the words from God that we speak out – like the lady on our prayer team who asked 'How is your daughter?' – can only be seen in retrospect.

That said, whenever we sense God revealing something to us through any of these means we must remember, as with any of the gifts of the Spirit, that we could be wrong. Revelation needs to be weighed. If we feel we have an important word for someone, we need to consider it carefully before passing it on. Sometimes God gives us insight into situations that we are meant to keep completely to ourselves, so that we can pray into them. At other times it is right to speak the word out. We need to operate the gifts with diligence and sensitivity, asking God for wisdom if we are unsure what to do with the revelation:

> 'If any of you lacks wisdom, he should ask God, who gives generously to all without finding fault, and it will be given to him.' (Jas. 1:5)

If as yet you have not been released in a particular spiritual gift, speak with your leaders and ministry team and ask them to pray for you. Though our ability to 'step out' and use the gifts most often comes in a time of need, God is more than willing to bless us in this area as we express our desire to be used by Him in a particular way. Each gift can be specifically prayed for, received in faith, and then humbly exercised, trusting God for the results. Many people are released in the gift of tongues through the laying on of hands with prayer, and the other gifts can be similarly imparted, as we read happened to Timothy (2 Tim. 1:6). Those involved in ministering healing should be regularly asking God to release in them the necessary gifts in ever increasing measure.

The Work of the Holy Spirit

The gifts of the Spirit are not the only aspects of His work that are important in this ministry. Other aspects of the Spirit's ministry that we must remember as a church commits itself to releasing healing ministry are:

- The Holy Spirit is our teacher in all things. *'But when he, the Spirit of truth, comes, he will guide you into all truth'* (John 16:13). Consequently, we can be sure that He will guide us in all the decisions we have to make over the right exercise of this ministry.
- The Holy Spirit glorifies Christ. *'He will bring glory to me by taking from what is mine and making it known to you'* (John 16:14). When the healing ministry is properly exercised, more people will recognise Jesus as Lord, be more grateful to Him for all that He has done for them, and be more passionate about serving Him.
- The Holy Spirit will come if we ask. *'If you then, though you are evil, know how to give good gifts to your children, how much more will your Father in heaven give the Holy Spirit to those who ask him!"* (Luke 11:13). If we ask, then the Father will give us the Spirit and His gifts to enable us to exercise this ministry.
- The Holy Spirit acts dynamically in the local church. *'Now to each one the manifestation of the Spirit is given for the common good . . . All these are the work of one and*

the same Spirit, and he gives them to each one, just as he determines' (1 Cor. 12:7,11). He is longing to be as generous to and through members of the Church today as He was then. The ministry of the gifts of the Spirit is for everyone's benefit – so this is not something to be feared but welcomed.

- The Holy Spirit has a part for everyone to play. *'The body is a unit, though it is made up of many parts; and though all its parts are many, they form one body'* (1 Cor. 12:12). Often when healing ministry is introduced, some in the church will be tempted to feel superior because they are being 'used by God', and others can be made to feel inferior because they have a less supernatural ministry. The Holy Spirit doesn't give everyone public and visible roles, but it is important for the church leaders to recognise this and to honour those who are engaging in less visible activities such as 'the gift of helping others' or mercy ministry. These are equally important in helping to make the kingdom of God good news. *'Each one should use whatever gift he has received to serve others, faithfully administering God's grace in its various forms'* (1 Pet. 4:10).

- The Holy Spirit still speaks to the Church today. *'He who has an ear, let him hear what the Spirit says to the churches'* (Rev. 2:7). If we were to go wrong or get our priorities wrong then the Lord is perfectly able to correct us today, just as he did the early Church.

The Fruit of the Spirit

It is vital that those committed to being involved in healing ministry understand the need to keep bearing the fruit of the Spirit in their lives.

> 'The fruit of the Spirit is love, joy, peace, patience, kind-
> ness, goodness, faithfulness, gentleness and self-control.'
> (Gal 5:22)

When the power and gifts of the Holy Spirit come upon
a church or an individual it is easy to be mesmerised by
the wonder and newness of these things. Sometimes
there is a consequent loss of focus on the need to be continuously changed so that we live lives of purity like
Jesus did.

The Corinthian church was gloriously open to the
gifts of the Holy Spirit, but seemingly wasn't always
using them wisely. Paul had to write in firm terms to
remind of them of the importance of only exercising
these gifts in the context of love.

> 'If I speak in the tongues of men and of angels, but have
> not love, I am only a resounding gong or a clanging cym-
> bal. If I have the gift of prophecy and can fathom all mys-
> teries and all knowledge and if I have a faith that can
> move mountains but have not love, I am nothing.' (1 Cor.
> 12:1–2)

Similarly, we need to ensure that we don't abuse the
grace gifts of God and remember that the 'foundation'
for their effective use has to be a character and personality that is being shaped, moulded and transformed by
the Holy Spirit to represent the likeness of Christ. As we
cooperate with God's work to bring us to maturity, here
we will find the wisdom and sensitivity to use His gifts
in a way that honours Him and is a blessing to others.

7

Under-girding Values

In the early Church, using the gifts of the Spirit when the church gathered for worship was something that had to be handled with care and subject to order:

> 'But everything should be done in a fitting and orderly way.' (1 Cor. 14:40)

Similarly, as we seek to practise the healing ministry today, there needs to be a clear understanding about how it will operate and how those authorised to minister are to exercise this ministry under the authority of the church's leadership.

Having too many rules runs the danger of killing the ministry – *'the letter kills . . .'* (2 Cor. 3:6) and we have found it better to express and share common values which are accepted by all those involved in the ministry. In this chapter I have included the values that we have found are most important to emphasise both in the church and in the lives of those who minister healing.

Each of these is something that the church should value together and that individuals should be personally committed to if they are to be part of a church's authorised team. If a church leader releases people into ministry who do not hold to the church's values they are setting up the possibility of future conflict and this will only grieve the Holy Spirit and damage the effectiveness of the healing ministry.

The Person and Work of Christ

A church first needs to honour the uniqueness of Jesus and His sacrificial work upon the cross, atoning for human sin and overcoming the works of the enemy. Jesus is the One who shows us, in a unique way, what God is really like. No one else has done or could do this:

> 'No one has ever seen God, but God the One and Only, who is at the Father's side, has made him known.' (John 1:18)

When we see Jesus so committed to healing the sick we know that God's heart, mind, will and strength is committed to healing. To deny this is to deny and dishonour the unique revelation of God that Jesus has given us. Anyone who studies the gospels and sees Jesus healing the sick, is seeing the eternal heartbeat of God:

> 'Jesus answered . . . Anyone who has seen me has seen the Father.' (John 14:9)

The character of God is no different today than it was in Jesus day. He is unchanging in His nature. He is equally committed to healing the sick today as He was then. Knowing this gives those ministering healing in His name confidence that He will act as they pray in faith in the name of Jesus.

Moreover, we are told that on the cross Jesus has over-come all the powers of darkness, which includes the power of sickness, suffering and death. It is for this rea-son that the prophet Isaiah was able to say,

> 'But he was pierced for our transgressions, he was crushed for our iniquities; the punishment that brought us peace was upon him, **and by his wounds we are healed**' (Isa. 53:5)

Some place their main emphasis, when speaking about and ministering healing, on the fact that it is readily available to us here and now in the cross. Their conclu-sion is that it can be 'claimed' and then experienced with an equal certainty of God giving it as the forgiveness of sins and eternal salvation. This does not seem to be implied by the text and there is no evidence in the New Testament that the early Christians believed this. It is bet-ter to say that the cross 'opens up' all the blessings of Heaven to us (Eph. 1:3) and we enter the kingdom of God only as a result of it. We can immediately be assured of our eternal salvation and our eternal healing, but we may have to wait for some time (even to the resurrection itself) before we experience the full wonder of either.

There is a danger in teaching people that healing belongs to them 'now' i.e. that they already possess it, just as they already possess their salvation. It means, in practice, that though you are sick, you are already 'healed' and ought to be thinking about living in and keeping that healing. Often the language used when teaching this view amounts to, 'God has made provision for your healing, now you must go and appropriate it.' The problem here is that this approach places the onus for healing on the person who wants to be healed, as the language of the healing minister becomes, 'Go away and claim your healing'. This approach fails for me both in its exegesis and its understanding of mortality.

In exegetical terms, we frequently see in Scripture prophets speaking about future events as though they were already in existence. '*A child is born, a son is given to us*' was expressed in the present tense, even though it was a distant future event, such was the clarity and certainty of the prophet's vision. The prophetic statement '*By his wounds we are healed*' then, can have both a present and future application.

On the issue of our mortality, we believe that both sickness and death are a result of the fall and that we need to be 'healed' from both. Why do we make the distinction between physical illness and our ultimate mortality when we apply the Isaiah text? If we could appropriate absolutely *everything* that God has for us *now* – as if it depended only on us – then surely we would be immortal already, and we obviously are not! The truth is, there are certain things that we will have to wait to experience when Jesus returns.

Instead we recognise that healing is a sovereign work of God that requires the divine intervention of the Holy Spirit. As we minister healing, we thank Jesus for His power to heal and for His death on the cross through which healing comes. In this way we both honour the Lord and build our faith and that of the person we are ministering to.

No one can be considered for this ministry who does not have a personal relationship with the Lord, having already experienced His forgiveness and regeneration. The more a person is conscious of what Jesus has done for them on the cross the more able they will be to minister the power of the cross to others.

More could be said about this, but I am assuming that most readers are already clear on the central place of

Jesus in their lives than on the significance of the other values we address now.

The Word of God

> 'All Scripture is God-breathed and is useful for teaching, rebuking, correcting and training in righteousness, so that the man of God may be thoroughly equipped for every good work.' (2 Tim. 3:16–17)

The Bible is our guidebook in every aspect of Christian life and ministry. It is through our study of the Bible, and as God reveals Himself to us through it, that we find our theology and model for healing ministry. All that it is written in this book must be tested against the Scriptures to demonstrate its truthfulness.

The Bible speaks to us of our authority for healing as we minister in the name of Jesus. We are not claiming any authority for ourselves in this generation which Bible-reading and believing Christians have not deduced previously. We are not 'discovering' a healing ministry, but *re-discovering* what the Bible tells us that Jesus entrusted to His first, prototype disciples.

The Bible reminds us of the context for healing: the preaching of the cross and the kingdom of God. Healing in Jesus' life always accompanied His proclamation of the good news of God's kingship, love and power. In the early Church, as the good news was taken from place to place, signs and wonders went alongside the proclamation of the gospel. Healing ministry must never replace the proclamation of the gospel – the two go hand in hand.

In 2005 Anne and I went on sabbatical to visit Heidi Baker in Mozambique. During this time we went with her and her teams on various evangelistic trips to villages at some distance from her bases in Maputo and Pemba. The normal format for these forays is to drive to these villages in a flat bed truck which then becomes the preaching platform. They then show the film 'Jesus', projected from a generator-driven film projector onto a huge screen on the back of the truck. In a village with no electricity this spectacle in itself can draw a huge crowd of highly interested people! An evangelist then preaches the good news of God's love in Jesus and invites people to come to Jesus for their salvation. This is followed by a call for the sick to come to Jesus for their healing. The team members, Anne and I included, were dispersed among the crowd and could pray for the sick around us as they asked us to. On one occasion Heidi said, 'I am going to talk to you about Jesus and call you to give your lives to Him; then we will pray for everyone who is sick. I want you to find anyone in the village who is deaf and, after I have preached, Jesus will heal them.' Anne and I looked at each other thinking, 'We have never heard an evangelistic address start like that in the UK', and I supposed that she must have had a word of knowledge from the Lord about what He wanted to do that night (she confirmed this to us when we talked with her later).

When she made her appeal for people to receive Jesus as their Saviour hundreds of people in this Muslim village put their hands up and prayed the prayer with her. By then a woman had brought her 11 year old deaf from birth daughter to the front of the crowd. Heidi asked some of her orphans to pray with her for a while and soon we heard a general hollering of joy and much stamping of feet and waving of hands. We were too far back to hear or see much and only got the details on the way back to her base. The girl's ears were opened and she could hear. To test this they asked her to repeat certain words which she couldn't say before; never having heard them she couldn't previously pronounce them. This is why so many deaf people are also severely speech impaired, just as she was. When they realised she could hear and repeat words in an understandable manner they taught her to say, 'Mum, I love you.' The shout of joy and praise to God was because the first words that her daughter spoke to her mother, 11 long years after her birth, in a clearly understandable manner were, 'Mum, I love you'. The whole extended family were weeping with joy (as were most of the praying team).

We must always seek to achieve a proper balance as we incorporate healing ministry into the life of the church. Not to do so means that other areas of life will suffer. About eighteen months into the outbreak of the Toronto Blessing in the UK, I realised that I had spent the best part of a year only praying for those people who came forward for prayer during ministry times. Eventually I realised, due to the fact that only a percentage of people will come forward, that I was neglecting a large proportion of the church. There were always those who stood back and observed what was happening. I was focusing my energies on the apparently spiritually hungry, and never engaging in conversation with these other people. Some of those 'at the back' of the church were literally on their way out of the door because I had lost relationship with them.

This was perhaps a unique period in the life of the church, but the principle still holds. Unless the church leader emphasises a proper balance in the life of the church, all the attention will be focused on a small number of people while other important aspects of church life go unaddressed.

The Bible gives us good models – that of Jesus in the gospels and the early Christians in the book of Acts. If we follow these models we will avoid getting out of balance. We will also avoid adopting any of the affectations or off-putting practices that some healing ministries can exhibit.

The Bible also warns us against abusing the gifts or falling prey to temptations such as greed:

> 'Simon said, "Give me also this ability so that everyone on whom I lay my hands may receive the Holy Spirit."' (Acts 8:19)

Those involved in this ministry should be committed to meditating on the Scriptures, asking God to speak through them, and to letting the Scriptures fashion all their attitudes and every aspect of their lifestyle, as well as forming their understanding and practise of the healing ministry.

Wholeness

It has been stated already, but bears repeating, that God is committed to our wholeness. Paul writes in 1 Thessalonians,

> 'May God himself, the God of peace, sanctify you through and through. May your whole spirit, soul and body be kept blameless at the coming of our Lord Jesus Christ.' (1 Thess. 5:23)

This word 'whole' is derived from the Greek word *sozo*. Used frequently in the gospels it is sometimes thought to refer simply to the idea of eternal salvation which God offers every individual through Christ (Matt. 1:21). But actually its meaning is much broader and includes such concepts as:

- Holiness. *'Make every effort to live in peace with all men and to be holy; without holiness no one will see the Lord'* (Heb. 12:14). Our sanctification is an integral part of our wholeness. In the Bible the command to be holy is frequently repeated, *'Be ye holy even as I am holy'* (1 Pet. 1:6). If a church is to be a place where the Holy Spirit is free to minister there must be a real commitment to purity and holiness.

- Unity. *'Make every effort to keep the unity of the Spirit through the bond of peace'* (Eph. 4:3). Harmonious, loving relationships are meant to be the hallmark of the Church. John wrote, *'By this all men will know that you are my disciples, if you love one another'* (John 13:35). When relationships are fragmented through unforgiveness, jealousy, competition and the like, the 'shalom' of the Christian community is destroyed and healing is inhibited.

- Maturity. *'Until we all reach unity in the faith and in the knowledge of the Son of God and become mature, attaining to the whole measure of the fullness of Christ'* (Eph. 4:13). Maturity in Christ means taking responsibility for our own acts, owning our bad decisions and no longer blaming others. Although we should always be childlike in our attitude, we should never be childish in our emotions and in our relationships.

- Healing. Sometimes the Greek word *sozo* is also used when Jesus healed sick people, or set the demonised free. So wholeness involves our coming to Jesus for healing too.

- Suffering. Our theology both for healing and suffering comes from our understanding that the kingdom of God is already present in part, but not yet fully here. Our primary example for living in these in-between times is Jesus who, *'learned obedience from what he suffered'* (Heb. 5:8). We need to have a good understanding of the present, partial nature of the kingdom of God and of the place of suffering in our lives, and that of others, if we are to go on believing in the goodness of God lifelong. This is the only way to avoid the despair that would otherwise overwhelm us as we live in a world in which there is so much untold suffering and injustice.

Consequently, those involved in ministering healing should be committed to growing in purity, to maintaining loving relationships, to maturing in every area of their lives, to receiving prayer for their own healing, and to learning how to respond in a Christlike manner to suffering and difficulty in their life.

> 'No discipline seems pleasant at the time, but painful. Later on, however, it produces a harvest of righteousness and peace for those who have been trained by it.' (Heb. 12:11)

Love For the Individual

Every individual person is of infinite value to God and we need to learn to view each person in the same way that God views them. We see that,

- God knows us all personally by name. *'He calls his own sheep by name and leads them out'* (John 10:3).
- God knows the number of hairs on our heads. *'And even the very hairs of your head are all numbered'* (Matt. 10:30).
- God measures our tears. *'Record my lament; list my tears on your scroll – are they not in your record?'* (Ps. 56:8).

On one notable occasion in the Bible, Jesus was prepared to stop everything because He noticed that someone in the crowd had touched His robe and that healing power had left Him (Luke 8:43–48). He was not prepared to go on without finding out who this person was and commending her.

In Luke 7 we find the story of a woman whose son has died. Jesus encountered her as she was in the very process of accompanying the funeral procession to bury his body. Moved with a deep compassion Jesus stepped in. Scripture tells us that *'His heart went out to them'* and the funeral was brought to an abrupt but joyous halt as He prayed and the boy was brought back to life. It is interesting that Jesus Himself took the initiative here. Neither the crowd nor the mother brought the boy to Him. His natural reaction to their pain and suffering was to empathise and reach out.

Such is Christ's care for the individual. We need to develop and express a similar sensitivity for each individual in our prayer ministry.

A good rule of thumb in ministry is not to do anything to someone else that we wouldn't like done to us! This simple principle will help us avoid much malpractice. In particular we need to learn to treat individuals . . .

- . . . with empathy and compassionate love. *'Love your neighbour as your self'* (Luke 10:25–37).
- . . . with a willingness to listen and take them seriously. *'Everyone should be quick to listen, slow to speak'* (Jas. 1:19).
- . . . with acceptance and without harsh judgement. *'Accept one another, then, just as Christ accepted you'* (Rom. 15:7).
- . . . with respect and dignity. *'In honour preferring one another'* (Rom. 12:10).

- . . . with humility and gentleness. *'Be completely humble and gentle; be patient, bearing with one another in love'* (Eph. 4:2).

It has been said, people don't care how much we know, they want to know how much we care. Nowhere is this more true than in healing ministry. A commitment to demonstrate the love of Christ to individuals and see them made whole is therefore essential.

One of the first people we prayed for when we launched healing on the streets was a lady named Margaret. She stopped for prayer and was powerfully touched, tears streaming down her face, as the presence of God came and He healed her. Following that experience she came along to our afternoon café style service, specially designed for those who are curious about Jesus, but perhaps not ready to come to 'normal' church. Then she began attending our Alpha course. Eventually she gave her life to Christ and now has a real, personal relationship with the Lord.

At no point did we pressurise or preach at Margaret. Our main concern was to minister the love and healing of God to her and allow the Holy Spirit to continue to work in her life from there. This ministry is not about expecting everyone to come to Christ, but about as many people as possible learning about the love of God. During that process, we expect that some will come to faith as a result. We have to realise that although many people will be touched by God as we pray for their healing, it may take an unchurched person a long time before they really understand and acknowledge God and come to true faith in Him.

A Word of Caution

In our efforts to maintain a balanced ministry we will no doubt be wary – especially in a church setting – of focusing too much attention on the same people all the time, especially if we feel that they may be attention seeking (by coming out for prayer far more than they need to). Whilst we should recognise this as a possibility and remind people to take responsibility for seeking and hearing from God personally, we must also exercise wisdom and discretion.

I once suspected a lady who frequently came forward for prayer of 'attention seeking' when in reality God was working in her life in a significant way. My suspicions were exacerbated by the fact that whenever she was prayed for she would manifest a lot of shaking and tended to fall over as soon as someone prayed for her. I wondered whether this was necessary and began to think of speaking to her about it, but despite my doubts I didn't feel God prompting me to intervene.

After this had gone on most Sundays for three or four months she came to me and said that God had been speaking to her about starting a ministry among unchurched elderly people in the community. At that point in the life of the church we had a very youthful congregation and the older members of society were definitely underrepresented. She outlined what she felt the Lord had told her to do and I agreed. She began this ministry and it grew very quickly. Within a year we had up to 50 people attending the elderly people's midweek group we arranged, and for special events at Easter and Christmas we gathered over 100 people. None of them were church attendees – they were ordinary people from the community that we had never previously reached. God had been preparing this lady for this ministry, despite her physical responses looking to me like attention-seeking and a distraction for others. So we must learn how to use discernment and love, trying to find out what is really happening below the surface before 'barging in' and potentially stopping the transforming work of the Holy Spirit!

The Body of Christ

The local church fellowship is the best place to learn how to minister healing. It is here that we are called to enter into loving and accountable relationships, both with our peers and those in leadership.

I realised early on that people would need both encouragement and training to become involved in healing ministry, so I would try to do both. I would invite individuals to come and pray alongside me as I prayed for others' healing. Most people respond better to this kind of personal invitation, rather than a public appeal, and it is an ideal way to help people grow in confidence and begin to minister to others.

It is also in our local church that we should have friends who are committed both to this healing ministry and to seeing us grow in maturity in Christ. These are the sort of friends who can correct us if we misuse the gifts. None of us particularly like being corrected – it is painful – but through it we grow and we learn that, 'Wounds from a friend can be trusted' (Prov. 27:6).

In the church there is also an appointed leadership who are accountable to God for the right ordering of the church's life and ministry. They want to ensure this healing ministry is exercised in a right way. Proper respect for the leadership of the church is to the advantage of everyone.

'Obey your leaders and submit to their authority. They keep watch over you as men who must give an account. Obey them so that their work will be a joy, not a burden, for that would be of no advantage to you.' (Heb. 13:17)

The leaders of a church must be committed themselves both to understanding and practicing healing ministry if it is to have the spiritual space to grow and blossom in the church. Leaders cannot say, 'I believe in this, but I'm not going to be involved in it' and then expect a burgeoning healing ministry to develop. Instead, leaders need to set a culture for healing in the church by being involved in it. This does not mean, if you are a leader, that you need to be part of the prayer ministry team at weekends or praying for people every day during the week, but you must be a practitioner as well as a supporter.

What this also does is create an environment in which the church leaders and those leading the healing ministry work closely together in relationship. Rather than there being a distance between the leadership and the healing ministry, there will be a cohesion and an accountability. This means there is much less chance of polarisation or that maverick practices will creep into the ministry.

A wise church leader will regularly review the practices of the team with the team leader to ensure that the guidelines and values to which the church ascribes are being adhered to. From time to time it may be necessary to speak to individuals on the team if they are departing from these practices and introducing other values. If this is not done, then over a period of time the ministry will dry up because people will no longer know how they will be ministered to if they come for prayer. Some sort of quality control needs to be exercised over the ministry offered.

Team members have to be willing to be accountable for their own spiritual life. It is possible that though someone may be highly gifted in prayer ministry, they are running away from other issues in their life or falling into temptation and sin. In such cases, it may be necessary to ask someone to stop being part of the team for a while until those issues are dealt with. I know of one church leader who was faced with a difficult issue with a male member of his church healing team. He was not a person who had many friends and he often stood isolated and alone in the church building after services watching others mixing socially over coffee. Then he attended the church's healing training days and really wanted to be part of the team. It was as if being part of the team gave him a role in church in a way that he hadn't felt previously. Unfortunately, after a while a number of women came to the church leader saying that they felt distinctly 'ill at ease' when he prayed with them (even though he abided by the church's rule and never prayed for women without another female member of the team being present). Some complained that he stood too close physically, and that he was invading their space, but there were no more definite complaints than that. The vicar spoke to him about these concerns, but despite giving him time to change it became apparent that the concerns of many women in the church remained.

The vicar was left with a difficult choice – should he let the man continue on the team, or should he ask him to step down? In the end he asked him to step down because he knew that the reputation of the ministry could be put in jeopardy – especially if the word spread that it was no longer safe to go forward for prayer at the end of the service because one of the team might pray over you inappropriately. Once that happened it wouldn't be long before people stopped coming forward for prayer at all. It is tempting to avoid the sort of conflict that this type of action can bring, but in my experience, failure to do this only brings the healing ministry into disrepute. Those involved in ministering healing must be people who are willing to follow the guidelines and values set by the church leadership, and who are open to the gentle correction of the church's leaders. To 'anticipate' such problems in the team, it is helpful for the church leader to host occasional ministry team meetings for feedback, revue, teaching, fresh empowering and the reiteration of values.

There is one other thing about ministering healing in the local church. As David Pytches says, 'The meeting place is the learning place for the marketplace.' We realise that God doesn't just want us to minister healing inside the church, but that we take His love and power into homes, hospitals, our places of work and anywhere where we might encounter those who are sick. To this end, how we conduct our healing ministry in the church is vital. What we do here – as Christians gather in the meeting place – will fundamentally determine what those same believers do in their daily 'marketplace' lives. For that reason we need to learn how to do this ministry effectively and in a non-religious way, so that we can confidently offer prayer to anyone, believer or not, anywhere, at any time. If, by contrast, we allow strange prayer practises to develop in the church then we will never successfully take this ministry into people's homes or onto the streets. Yet this is where Jesus did it in His day and where He wants us to take His healing today.

Prayer

God has bound Himself to certain principles regarding the way He works in His world. Although He is Almighty, He has chosen to work through weak and mortal human beings. It seems as if the weaker and more childlike we are, the more He is glorified.

> 'But we have this treasure in jars of clay to show that this all-surpassing power is from God and not from us.' (2 Cor. 4:7)

God has promised that He will answer the prayers of His people. He has bound Himself to hear and respond to those who wholeheartedly seek Him.

> 'You will seek me and find me when you seek me with all your heart.' (Jer. 29:13)

This is true for individuals who call upon Him for themselves and also for churches who call upon Him together, asking that their church might become a vibrant, life-giving and healing community such as the first Church was.

There are four important applications for this in the realm of prayer for healing:

1. It is true for individuals who come forward for prayer as they earnestly seek God. We need to encourage people to pray for their own healing, not just to come and be prayed for by others. The kingdom of God advances as people seize it: *'From the days of John the Baptist until now, the kingdom of heaven has been forcefully advancing, and forceful men lay hold of it'* (Matt. 11:12).

2. It is true for those ministering as they earnestly pray for each person they are called to minister to. It is all too easy to stop a time of ministry prematurely, before the healing comes. Who knows what might happen if we are prepared to give more time. '*And the prayer offered in faith will make the sick person well; the Lord will raise him up*' (Jas. 5:15).

3. It is also true in preparation for prayer ministry. If anyone wants to become more effective in this healing ministry they must learn the disciplines of prayer and be prepared at times to fast in preparation for some types and times of ministry. '*After Jesus had gone indoors, his disciples asked him privately, "Why couldn't we drive it out?" He replied, "This kind can come out only by prayer and fasting."*' (see Mark 9:29 footnote)

4. A church that wants to see this ministry flourish should commit itself to praying that God will give them courage to keep declaring the truth that, 'Our God reigns and has power to heal', and to keep asking God to perform signs and wonders amongst them: '*Now, Lord, consider their threats and enable your servants to speak your word with great boldness. Stretch out your hand to heal and perform miraculous signs and wonders through the name of your holy servant Jesus*' (Acts 4:29–30).

A church that is committed to praying for God to release His healing power will, over time, see that beginning to happen. God can do it and does do it wherever His people ask Him! (Jas. 4:2)

8

The Place of Faith

The Significance of Faith

Faith seems to be the purest conductor of the power of God. It brings the power of God to the point of need. On numerous occasions when Jesus healed the sick He commented on the role that faith played in creating an environment in which healing could flow. Some examples are:

- The woman who had been bleeding for twelve years, who pushed through the crowd to touch the hem of Jesus' garment. 'Jesus turned and saw her . . . *"Your faith has healed you." And the woman was healed from that moment'* (Matt. 9:22).
- The woman whom Jesus forgave. *'Jesus said to the woman, "Your faith has saved you; go in peace"'* (Luke 7:50).
- One of the ten lepers who were healed. *'Then he said to him, "Rise and go; your faith has made you well"'* (Luke 17:19).

Faith must be important, since there wasn't a single occasion when Jesus said, 'Your unbelief has made you well'! He also, on at least one occasion, asked those seeking healing whether they believed He could do it:

> 'When he had gone indoors, the blind men came to him, and he asked them, "Do you believe that I am able to do this?" "Yes, Lord," they replied' (Matt. 9:28).

So we need to learn to pray the prayer, 'I do believe; help me overcome my unbelief!' (Mark 9:24).

What Does Faith Look Like?

If we need to respond to faith as Jesus did then it's important to know how to recognise faith. Interestingly, it is exhibited in some very different ways. Most of us find it is easier to recognise faith expressed in some of these ways than others.

- In some people faith is expressed very quietly and unobtrusively, such that most people, the original disciples included, would not be able to recognise it as faith. The woman who pushes her way through the crowd to touch the hem of Jesus' robes is one of these.

  > 'Just then a woman who had been subject to bleeding for twelve years came up behind him and touched the edge of his cloak. She said to herself, "If I only touch his cloak, I will be healed." Jesus turned and saw her. "Take heart, daughter," he said, "your faith has healed you." And the woman was healed from that moment.' (Matt. 9:20–22)

- In some people faith is expressed noisily and exuberantly, and could be mistaken for emotionalism, as in the case of blind Bartimaeus.

'When he heard that it was Jesus of Nazareth, he began
to shout, "Jesus, Son of David, have mercy on me!"
Many rebuked him and told him to be quiet, but he
shouted all the more, "Son of David, have mercy on
me!". . . "What do you want me to do for you?" Jesus
asked him. The blind man said, "Rabbi, I want to see."
"Go," said Jesus, "your faith has healed you."
Immediately he received his sight and followed Jesus
along the road.' (Mark 10:47–52)

- In others faith is expressed through a type of reasoning
  process, easily dismissed as intellectualism. This was
  how the Centurion's faith was expressed to Jesus.

'The centurion sent friends to say to Jesus: "Lord, don't
trouble yourself, for I do not deserve to have you come
under my roof. That is why I did not even consider
myself worthy to come to you. But say the word, and my
servant will be healed. For I myself am a man under
authority, with soldiers under me. I tell this one, 'Go,'
and he goes; and that one, 'Come,' and he comes. I say to
my servant, 'Do this,' and he does it." When Jesus heard
this, he was amazed at him, and turning to the crowd
following him, he said, "I tell you, I have not found such
great faith even in Israel."' (Luke 7:6–9)

- In others faith is expressed through active commitment to meeting Jesus personally, even when it is
  difficult to do so. The faith of the friends of the para-
  plegic is visible through their dangerous foray onto
  and then through the roof of the house, in order to
  lower the stretcher at Jesus' feet.

'Since they could not get him to Jesus because of the
crowd, they made an opening in the roof above Jesus and,

after digging through it, lowered the mat the paralyzed man was lying on. When Jesus saw their faith, he said to the paralytic, "Son, your sins are forgiven."' (Mark 2:4–5)

Who Has to Exercise Faith?

From the above examples we see that on some occasions the person who comes asking for prayer is the person who is exercising faith, and whom Jesus commends, as in the case of the two blind men:

'Then he touched their eyes and said, "According to your faith will it be done to you."' (Matt. 9:29)

On other occasions some friend or friends of the suffering person are the ones who take the initiative in coming to Jesus, and it is them who Jesus commends. One example is when the Canaanite woman comes asking for Jesus to heal her daughter:

'Then Jesus answered, "Woman, you have great faith! Your request is granted." And her daughter was healed from that very hour.' (Matt. 15:28)

On other occasions Jesus appeared to be the only one who believed that God could bring healing. At the raising of Lazarus Martha and Mary seem to have had a vague belief that God was powerful, but it didn't stretch to raising the dead back to life on Earth. In their eyes Lazarus had reached a stage beyond the reach of faith! So it is left to Jesus to turn to God in faith and say,

'"Take away the stone." "But, Lord," said Martha . . . "by this time there is a bad odour, for he has been there four

days" ... they took away the stone ... then Jesus looked
up and said, "Father, I thank you that you have heard me
... Lazarus, come out!" ... The dead man came out.'
(John 11:39–44)

I heard a story of a similar nature from one of our recent
New Wine conferences.

A lady called Caroline had suffered from a stroke in
2001, followed by a series of mini-strokes. Then, in
March 2007 she was diagnosed with a brain tumour.
After undergoing intensive radiotherapy treatment she
then discovered that the treatment itself had caused
severe nerve damage that resulted in a loss of balance
and her gradual deterioration to becoming dependent
on a walking stick and, then occasionally the need for a
wheelchair.

She came to New Wine with her husband and a group
of friends and was excited to be out and about after long
periods confined to the house. But she described herself
as being something of a 'target' for healing ministry and
not always in the most sensitive or helpful of ways. So it
was that she attended the evening meeting, in her wheelchair, with little or no expectation of God healing her.

Her faith and her relationship with God was at an all
time low. She trusted God for her future and told herself
that she didn't need to be healed physically to be a
whole person, but at the same time felt she was in a
'spiritual desert'. Whenever there was a time of worship
she would 'sing' rather than 'praise', had only the
briefest of conversations with God and had all but given
up reading her Bible. That night she sat through the worship going through the motions.

A line in a song said, 'You heal all my diseases'. At
that moment she thought to herself, 'You've not healed
mine! But I trust You anyway.' Seconds later she felt a

power pass through her body from the top to the bottom and with it came a feeling of complete and utter certainty: 'I'm healed!' Seconds later, she heard the almost audible voice of God say, 'If you want to go to the front and dance, you can!' Instead, suddenly aware that she needed the bathroom, she decided to test her legs by going to find it. She found herself able to walk, unaided, through the crowd, out onto the uneven roadway, up steps, down steps and back into the meeting.

At no point did she ask for healing or, to her knowledge, have anyone pray for her healing on this day. God simply arrived in the atmosphere of praise and worship and chose to heal her, despite her lack of expectations. Later that evening her wheelchair was folded away and placed in the boot of their car! When she arrived back home after New Wine her whole community were immediately aware of the power of God to heal today.

The Faith of the Person Ministering

As the Lord Jesus entrusted this ministry to His disciples He said,

> 'I tell you the truth, anyone who has faith in me will do what I have been doing. He will do even greater things than these, because I am going to the Father.' (John 14:12)

Those ministering must do all that they can to grow in their faith in Jesus. It seems as if sometimes healing doesn't come as a result of the lack of faith of those praying:

> 'Then the disciples came to Jesus in private and asked, "Why couldn't we drive it out?" He replied, "Because you have so little faith."' (Matt. 17:19–20)

It is probably as much the *type* of faith required as the *size* of faith that is important, for Jesus continues,

> 'I tell you the truth, if you have faith as small as a mustard seed, you can say to this mountain, "Move from here to there" and it will move. Nothing will be impossible for you.' (Matt. 19:20)

In practise people often have faith for different things. Some have faith for evangelism and know they can easily lead others into the kingdom. Others have faith for money and can easily give their money away to the poor because they know God will always supply their needs. Others have faith for healing and are certain that as they minister healing the sick will be healed. God wants us to exercise faith in a number of different areas of life and ministry, and not just in one of them. Moreover, we can grow and develop our faith for healing just as we can grow our faith for any of these other things.

Faith is important, but in the Bible we never see Jesus *blaming* individuals or *accusing* them of a lack of faith resulting in a lack of healing. It is we who think in such terms, not God, because we live in a culture that likes to identify a cause and effect for every situation. We too readily look for an underlying cause as to why someone is not healed because we find it difficult to live with paradox. We want to know what's to blame! But despite our need to have an explanation for everything, God doesn't always give it. Therefore, in our praying for others, we should always make the invitation for them to return for more prayer. We must make it easy for people to come to God for healing, rather than looking for reasons or creating barriers that say to people, in effect, 'Only come back when you have more faith!'

How Does Faith Grow?

When Paul writes to Timothy as the leader of the church in Ephesus, he says that faith is something that should be pursued, implying that alongside other aspects of our Christian lives it can grow.

> 'Flee the evil desires of youth, and pursue righteousness, faith, love and peace.' (2 Tim. 2:22)

How can faith grow? It grows . . .

1. Through hearing. *'Consequently, faith comes from hearing the message, and the message is heard through the word of Christ'* (Rom. 10:17). As we read the gospel stories we see God's total commitment to healing the sick. God's character hasn't changed – He is as committed to healing today as He was then. If we immerse ourselves in the stories in the gospels of what Jesus did during His physical life on earth, our faith in Him will grow. We can also read, listen to, and even watch via the Internet other stories of what He is still doing through His Body, the Church, around the world today. Testimonies always build faith.

2. Through seeing. *'Believe me when I say that I am in the Father and the Father is in me; or at least believe on the evidence of the miracles themselves'* (John 14:11). We need to deliberately go to places, churches and conferences, where the sick are being healed today. 'Seeing is believing', or at least, seeing *helps* believing. As we witness God at work with our own eyes it is far easier to believe it in our hearts and spirits.

3. Through doing. *'If a man's gift is prophesying, let him use it in proportion to his faith'* (Rom. 12:6). We don't

need to have a lot of faith to start using the spiritual gifts and ministering healing. God has, *'hidden these things from the wise and learned, and revealed them to little children'* (Luke 10:21). To my understanding, just as a muscle is strengthened and grows through use, so too does our faith. But just as a muscle atrophies through lack of use, faith can wither if we don't exercise it. Consequently, Paul instructed these Christians to keep exercising their faith and keep prophesying.

4. Through persevering in difficult times. *'Let us fix our eyes on Jesus, the author and perfecter of our faith'* (Heb. 12:2). Just as Jesus brings us to faith in the first place, He is also committed to growing our faith within us. This growth sometimes comes through difficulties in our lives. These trials, or tests of our faith are sent by God to refine and develop our faith:

> 'These [trials] have come so that your faith – of greater worth than gold, which perishes even though refined by fire – may be proved genuine and may result in praise, glory and honour when Jesus Christ is revealed.' (1 Pet. 1:7)

Most individuals and churches that start to minister healing do not find the learning process easy or unopposed. God uses these difficult times to test our determination to become more like Jesus in this, as in every other aspect of ministry.

Those involved in ministering healing need to keep growing their experience and faith in God in these different ways if they are to become more effective in this ministry.

The Faith Environment

On three occasions in the gospels it appears as if an unbelieving environment can exercise a restraining power over the working of signs and wonders. When a father brings his demonised boy to the disciples for healing they are unable to set him free. When Jesus rejoins them, however, on His return from the Mount of Transfiguration, He says,

> 'O unbelieving and perverse generation . . . how long shall I stay with you? How long shall I put up with you?' (Matt. 17:17)

When Jesus is visiting His home town and it appears as if He is unable to work miracles there as freely as elsewhere, the explanation given is the lack of faith of its inhabitants.

> 'He could not do any miracles there, except lay his hands on a few sick people and heal them. And he was amazed at their lack of faith.' (Mark 6:5–6)

When a blind man is brought to Him in Bethsaida Jesus takes him out of town to heal him, and then warns him not to go home through Bethsaida (Mark 8:22–26). It seems as if the reason for this was that the town had already been given the opportunity to respond to the gospel, but had instead hardened their hearts (Luke 10:13–14). Jesus was aware that their hardness to the gospel could make the village a difficult place in which to heal or be healed.

In our day, a whole nation can be affected by the predominant attitude of its leader or its opinion formers. In cultures around the world where there is a ready understanding and belief in the supernatural, such as Singapore, it seems that local churches find it relatively easy to engage in effective healing ministry. By contrast, in the Western world, dominated until recently by a scientific rational world view in which the supernatural has so often been scorned, it is relatively difficult to start teaching and practising this ministry.

I have found that visiting the church in the developing world has been a great learning experience for me in the healing ministry. In Africa there is still a latent belief in a 'higher power'; the question isn't so much about whether there is a God, as we might argue in the West, but about what is the name of that God and how His power can be sought and brought to bear on people's lives. So the practise of witchcraft and the occult is still evident in many places, and when people who cannot afford medicine are sick they will go to the 'god' with the greatest power in search of healing. They have 'faith'; the issue is whether their faith is in the God and Father of our Lord Jesus. When they turn in faith to Him, rather than any other god, healing often comes quickly and easily.

When Anne and I were in Mozambique we had a number of examples of this. One evening after the evangelistic message the preacher called people to give their lives to Jesus. That night there was very little response to this call for salvation, but nonetheless he went on to ask the sick to come for healing. We found ourselves talking to a young man who told us that his limp, which we had immediately noticed as he came forward, was as a result of unhealed damage to his knee caused when he fell out of a tree some years earlier; he was in considerable pain whenever he walked. His teenage friends were sceptically egging him (and us!) on; they obviously didn't really believe that Jesus had power to heal and were humouring us. We prayed for all we were worth, and then asked him to try walking to see if there was any improvement. It was clear to us all there wasn't any at all – the pain was undiminished and the limp was as obvious as ever. We asked if we could pray again, and as we did so I felt the Lord nudging me to get him to ask for his own healing. So working through the interpreter I said, 'I would like you to ask Jesus to heal your knee – you have probably never asked Jesus to do anything for you before, but it's important for you to take His name on your lips and ask Him yourself.' I sensed that if he did this it would be real step of faith for him, with his Muslim upbringing, speaking to our Lord Jesus.

Falteringly, he said, 'Jesus, I've come to you today and I am asking you to heal my knee please.' As he said this aloud in front of his friends an immediate stillness came over them; it was as if the Lord Himself had suddenly arrived and banished their scepticism. Anne and I prayed again, in what was now an environment of faith, and soon felt we should ask him to try walking again. He gingerly began to walk away from us, then length-ened his stride, soon turning to run back towards us, to gasps of astonishment from his friends. He declared himself pain free and healed by Jesus. Then he began excitedly to ask our Mozambican hosts about how he could get to know this Jesus better, and whether there was a church he could go to. His friends too were delighted to hear that the lorry would stop in their vil-lage on Sunday to take them the dozen or so miles to the church in Pemba the following Sunday!

I told the story earlier of a deaf girl of 11 who was healed on another evening in Mozambique. After she had been healed in front of the whole crowd, Anne and I were particularly amazed at the speed at which other people began to be healed, saying that their headaches and stomach pains were taken away, or that they could move parts of their body without pain in a way they could not previously. It seemed as if this was a real environment of faith where it was not difficult for Jesus to do many wonderful healings. Being in that sort of climate of faith, even for a short time, gave us a greater awareness of how significant it is to try to build communities of faith. In the Western world some places, such as Lourdes, have historical reputations for this. But God is now building new communities as places of healing today. A good recent example is Ffald-y-Brenin in Pembrokeshire, about which a book, *The Grace Outpouring*, was written in 2008. It describes some remarkable physical and emotional healings as people have visited this centre of prayer and been overwhelmed by the presence of God, sometimes even without anyone praying for them directly!

The history of a particular nation or local church can also have a big impact on the present population or congregation. Church leaders therefore need to be sensitive to this history as well as being careful that in their preaching, and in the way they live their lives, they are imparting faith, rather than doubt to their church members.

Having said all these things about the need to keep building conscious faith, I know of various cases where people have been healed while they had little or no faith, either before or after they were healed. Similarly, those ministering may think they have had little or no faith. But God is sovereign and He is able to heal whomever and whenever He chooses to do so. We will often be surprised by the way His amazing grace reaches far beyond our expectations, faith and skill levels!

As we continue to seek to minister His love and healing to others, the values discussed above will act like lighthouses. If we keep focused on them and trust God, we will avoid any shipwrecks in this ministry.

Part 3

Specific Types of Healing Prayer

Introduction

As we engage in this type of ministry, week by week people will respond and ask for prayer. Many will want prayer for some physical ailment, but they may have other needs as well. In the next few chapters advice is provided on how to pray for these wider needs.

It is relatively easy, once you have received some basic training, to pray for healing. But many believers have never prayed to lead someone to Jesus. For that reason the next short chapter covers this topic. It will be helpful for any person who is part of a healing ministry team to have a basic understanding of how to lead someone to faith in Christ. Healing is often the thing which attracts someone to Christ and can be the key to them seeking and receiving Him as Lord of their life.

Some people who ask for prayer will have a greater need for emotional healing underlying their physical problems. Frequently, this has to do with the issue of unforgiveness. Chapter 10 deals specifically with this issue and explains how we should pray.

In Chapter 11 we look at how to pray for someone to be filled with the Holy Spirit. It is important for us to have some guidance on how to pray for this, since we want to be able to respond to those who are seeking more than just healing and want to go deeper in their relationship with the Lord.

Following on from this, Chapter 12 deals with the issue of deliverance and provides guidance on handling prayer ministry cases where the cause of sickness is demonic. Finally, Chapter 13 provides some guidelines for pastoral prayer ministry, sometimes called inner healing, which involves longer term ministry to individuals who need it.

9

Leading Someone to Christ

As you speak to a person who has expressed a desire to come to Christ, seek to discern what they are responding to. Verify if this is a first time commitment or the latest one of many. If it is the latter, it may be that what is needed is a scriptural basis for assurance, and/or the release of the Holy Spirit in their lives. Ascertain if the person is just being moved emotionally with little understanding of what receiving Christ means, or whether, on the other hand, they have come to this decision to give their life to Christ after some time of thinking and preparation.

There is no fixed formula for leading a person to Christ. We have to be open to the leading of the Spirit and listen and respond carefully to what the person is saying. It is helpful to keep some basic stepping stones in mind as you lead a person in prayer, but don't be bound by the order.

For a person to commit their life to Jesus Christ they normally have to be ready to do a number of things. This is a simple ABCD approach, which can be a helpful guideline for those who are unfamiliar with praying for salvation.

Admit Their Need

The person first needs to acknowledge their sinful state and admit their need of a Saviour. Ultimately this is the need for forgiveness from a Holy God who is our Judge.

> 'For all have sinned and fall short of the glory of God.' (Rom. 3:23)

> 'For the wages of sin is death.' (Rom. 6:23)

Sin is universal; it has spoilt us and separated us from God. The chasm is so great that it cannot be bridged from man's side. Sometimes a person may not be very articulate about this alienation from God or their need for forgiveness, but the Holy Spirit has made them aware that 'something' is either missing or wrong, or that their life is really in a mess of their own making and that the solution to their need is found in Jesus.

Believe in Christ

We can explain to the person that God is longing to bring each of us back into the loving relationship with Him for which He created us. He does this through sending His Son, Jesus, to take our sin and all its consequences in our place.

> 'God so loved the world [i.e. us] that He gave His one and only Son that whoever believes in Him shall not perish but have eternal life.' (John 3:16)

> 'For Christ died for sins, once for all, the righteous for the unrighteous, to bring you to God.' (1 Pet. 3:18)

Some people may not be really aware that *only* Jesus could do and has done this, but the Holy Spirit is able to bring someone to the awareness of His uniqueness over time. I am sure that most of the first disciples started to follow Jesus before they became aware of His uniqueness as the sin-bearing Saviour of the world. It was only through later reflection on their experience, through frequently listening to Jesus' teaching, and through the Holy Spirit deepening their understanding that they realised this. In leading people to make this life-changing decision we need to be careful not to create too many hurdles for them to jump before they can even start to follow Jesus. On one occasion He Himself refrains from telling His disciples everything and said that He would leave the Holy Spirit to teach them more in the future:

> 'I have much more to say to you, more than you can now bear. But when he, the Spirit of truth, comes, he will guide you into all truth.' (John 16:12–13)

Commit, Confess, Change

Committing one's life to Christ must involve the confessing and renouncing of all known sin and the willingness to commit to a lifetime of allowing God to change us from the inside out by his Holy Spirit.

> 'Jesus said to them all: "If anyone would come after me, he must deny himself and take up his cross daily and follow me. For whoever wants to save his life will lose it, but whoever loses his life for me will save it.' (Luke 9:23–24)

It doesn't matter how relatively good or sinful a life a person has lived up till this point; the issue is their willingness to admit they have been living the wrong way without Jesus, and their willingness to change direction – to call on His help and be changed from now on.

Declare Their Faith to Others

In the New Testament there is no such thing as a secret believer. New believers were normally immediately publicly baptised, joined the church, and were then required to bear witness to their faith:

> 'If you confess with your mouth, "Jesus is Lord," and believe in your heart that God raised him from the dead, you will be saved.' (Rom. 10:9)

If a person is willing to become known as a Christian immediately, it usually means they are now ready and serious about giving their life to Christ. If they are not willing, they may not be ready.

One way of leading a person through this process is by asking them questions such as these:

- Do you realise your need of Jesus?
- Do you realise that God loves you so much that He has done everything to forgive you and save you by sending Jesus to die and rise again for you?
- Do you realise that Jesus would have done this for you had you been the only sinner alive in the world?
- Are you willing to confess your sin and have your life changed?
- Are you willing to be known as a Christian?

If so, tell them God is wanting them to give their life to Christ now. The only question is would they like to do so?

Prayer

Ask if you can pray a prayer with them. Ask them to confess their sin in a simple prayer, to declare their belief in Jesus, to ask Him to come into their life by His Holy Spirit, and to ask Him to change them and help them to live as a Christian for the rest of their life.

Some people may be able to articulate this prayer for themselves. For others you may need to pray it aloud sentence by sentence, asking them to repeat each phrase after you. Some may take some time over different parts, depending on the extent of the convicting work of the Spirit.

If a person does this, then thank the Lord Jesus that He has now come into the person's life and assure them that Jesus has promised He will never leave them.

Filling With the Holy Spirit

Finish by asking if you can pray for them to be filled with the Spirit to know the joy of having Jesus in their life and to be strengthened to live for Him every day. If they consent, gently lay hands on them and ask the Holy Spirit to fill them. Pray silently in tongues over them and aloud asking God to give them more of His Spirit of righteousness, joy and peace. If the new Christian is obviously responding to the coming of the Holy Spirit then you may feel it appropriate to encourage them to pray in tongues as well. The sooner they do this the better.

Follow Up

Your ability to follow up the person may depend upon whether you are in your home church, at a conference, or in a faith-sharing situation. It is generally very helpful to share some of your own testimony as to how you personally follow Jesus Christ in your prayer life, in reading the Scriptures, and in fellowship and service to others in a local church.

Introduce them to the idea of reading the Scriptures for themselves so that they can see that these things are true. You could, for instance, give them Mark's Gospel and describe the best way of reading it. If you can give them a booklet such as *Why Jesus?* by Nicky Gumbel, this will also help them to become assured in the prayer and decision they have made.

It is also a good idea to say a little about the spiritual battle (temptation, etc) that they will encounter and the way in which they can overcome any doubts that the enemy might throw at them over the next few days. Don't overdo this, but a little warning is very helpful.

Encourage the new Christian to make contact with a local church and even to get in touch with a church minister. The minister should be able to introduce these new converts to some kind of beginners' group, such as an Alpha Course, etc.

10

Ministering Forgiveness

Many Christians live many years of their Christian lives harbouring secret feelings of shame and guilt which gnaw away at their spiritual vitality and make them relatively ineffective believers. If this is a result of their own sin, they need to know the reality of God's forgiveness. If this is as a result of sin committed against them, they need to experience release from that trauma. Key to this is that they are released from any unforgiveness they may hold towards the perpetrator of the sin. While at the heart of the Christian faith lies an awareness of the complete forgiveness Jesus offers to anyone who turns to Him, recognising that this has been won for them though Jesus' death on the cross, many Christians still only understand this forgiveness in a sort of legal sense. They realise that once they were 'guilty sinners' and now they are 'forgiven saints', but they haven't experienced the emotional power of this forgiveness setting them free from the shame of their sins. What we are talking about is the full appropriation of the forgiveness of Jesus, so that mind, heart, spirit, and body are set free from the guilt and shame of sin.

In the interview stage of praying for a person, if they mention that they have been abused in the past, it is very likely that they will need to release forgiveness to the perpetrator(s) of their abuse. It is relevant to ask, 'Have you been able to forgive the person who did this?' or 'That must have been so painful for you. How do you feel about that person now?' It is possible that the person has trapped themselves by making a vow at some stage, e.g. by saying, 'I will never forgive them for that' and you will need to help them pray through this and release forgiveness.

If people are reluctant to forgive we can gently point out this truth to them: those who abuse us are generally either ignorant of the fact that they have done so, or, have done so deliberately and consciously. In both cases the person will probably not be troubled in their conscience by the fact that you don't want to forgive them. The person most affected by unforgiveness is the person holding onto it. As someone once said, 'Deciding not to forgive someone is like taking poison yourself and hoping the other person dies.' Unforgiveness is terribly damaging and debilitating to the person harbouring it. We need to understand that expressing forgiveness to those who have hurt us is never about 'letting them off' as R.T. Kendall puts it or about saying that what they did doesn't matter. Rather its purpose is to free the individual who was abused and prevent them from continuing to suffer from that hurt for the rest of their life. As John Arnott says, 'Our bodies are not made to carry unforgiveness – if we hold onto unforgiveness then our bodies will break down.' If we hang onto it, unforgiveness eats away at us. When we have been hurt, our natural inclination is to want mercy for ourselves and judgement, or even punishment for the other person – but ultimately we have to trust that God will administer justice to all in His own time.

One word of caution needs to be expressed here. If you, as the healing minister, feel or discern that someone has been abused in the past – even though they have not said that – it can often be very counter-productive to mention it. It is always far better to allow the person themselves to disclose such information as and when they are ready to do so. Our role is simply to keep working with the person until they are ready to talk about their issues. If, clearly a person is in tension and turmoil as we are ministering to them, a safer approach is to ask them, 'What is going on inside of you right now?' Quite often they respond by saying they are having an inner battle, or that they want to say something but don't know if they dare say it. Here a non-judgemental attitude becomes very important, and this is something that I believe can and should be cultivated by those involved in this ministry. This is done first by really addressing the darkest side of our life, facing up to the realities of our own sin and frailty, and ensuring that we ourselves have brought that shame and guilt to the cross of Jesus and found His acceptance and forgiveness. This is the basis of accepting others – first we must,

> 'Accept one another, then, just as Christ accepted you.'
> (Rom. 15:7)

Second, the more aware we are personally of God's kindness towards us, the more we are able to offer the same kindness to others. There is a glorious phrase in Paul's letter to the Romans which captures the power of kindness:

> 'God's kindness leads you towards repentance.' (Rom. 2:14)

When the judgemental Pharisees brought to Jesus a woman whom they had caught committing adultery, they waited to see how He would express God's judgement. He doodled in the sand, perhaps in embarrassment, and perhaps also waiting for His Father to give Him the spiritual gift of a word of wisdom. It seems they were frustrated by the delay:

> 'When they kept on questioning him, he straightened up and said to them, "If any one of you is without sin, let him be the first to throw a stone at her. Again he stooped down and wrote on the ground. At this, those who heard began to go away one at a time, the older ones first, until only Jesus was left, with the woman still standing there. Jesus straightened up and asked her, "Woman, where are they? Has no-one condemned you?" "No one, sir," she said. "Then neither do I condemn you," Jesus declared. "Go now and leave your life of sin."' (John 8:7–11)

One might think, 'How on earth could a woman like that change her ways?' The answer Jesus gives is through an experience of God's extraordinary kindness and complete forgiveness (and not as the Pharisees might have supposed in some rigid law enforcement of God's punishment).

Third, we need to develop ways of helping people to articulate their inner pain aloud. For instance, it may well be they fear their confession will affect their future relationship with us so I say something like, 'This matter is between you and Jesus. I will hear what you tell me, but I won't remember it.' In my case that is an entirely honest thing and increasingly so as the years go by, and as I pray for more and more people! This fear is perhaps the reason that some people make confessions to other Christians at conferences where they are unknown and in front of people with whom they will have no continuing relationship.

However we phrase it, we need people to know that they are at liberty to disclose everything necessary to achieve their healing, and that we will not condemn them, whatever they confess.

Helping Someone Receive Forgiveness

Sometimes people need to confess their sin to the Lord out loud, in front of others, in order to receive their healing from past shame:

> 'Therefore confess your sins to each other and pray for each other so that you may be healed.' (Jas. 5:16)

Some people will be willing to do this aloud, but others may be too embarrassed to, in which case we need to give them space for a silent confession. At the same time we encourage them to renounce sinful practises in the future. When they have finished praying we use the authority we have been given to minister forgiveness in the name of Jesus:

> 'If you forgive anyone his sins, they are forgiven; if you do not forgive them, they are not forgiven.' (John 20:23)

It can sometimes be helpful to:

- Declare Scripture over the person. For instance, 'God says *"If we confess our sins, he is faithful and just and will forgive us our sins and purify us from all unrighteousness."'* (1 John 1:9)

- Proclaim forgiveness e.g. 'As a servant of Jesus I proclaim that whatever you have confessed is now forgiven by the blood of Jesus.'

- Pronounce a cleansing with Jesus' blood: 'I pour the blood of Jesus over you (or a part of the body that has been involved in the sin), which cleanses you from all sin and washes whiter than snow.'

I first came across this way of praying in a conference in California at a Vineyard church. I had asked for prayer for certain things in my life for which I was finding it hard both to be assured of God's forgiveness, and I certainly was unable to forgive myself also. After making a confession and weeping before the Lord those praying for me prayed in this vein. I then had an almost tangible physical awareness of an oil-like substance poured over me from head to foot which left me feeling totally cleansed on the inside and the outside, just like a new man. I believe this is what 'cleansing with the blood of Jesus' is meant to effect.

Not long after that I was praying with a woman who had confessed committing adultery. She was taking responsibility and confessing it as sin. I could see from her tears and her attitude that this was a godly sorrow that would lead to a life of repentance (2 Cor. 7:10), so I said, 'I take the blood of Jesus and pour it over you to cleanse you from all sin' and waited for a few minutes as she trembled and wept further. Then her face was broken by a wonderful smile and there was an almost translucent radiance upon her. Her first words when I asked her what was happening were, 'Where is the bucket?' Her experience of a cleansing liquid being poured over her was so definite that it seemed to her more real than imaginary! She became a changed woman thereafter.

- Sign with the cross: 'I sign you with the cross as an assurance that whatever you have confessed is now forgiven by the blood of Jesus on the cross.'

Always give the Holy Spirit time to take the words and apply them to the person's spirit. Allow the person time to enjoy the relief of having their inner spirit cleansed from the sin, shame and accusation of the enemy. If a person has confessed sin and received the assurance of their forgiveness it is good to help them to know how to avoid that temptation again.

Finish this time with a prayer of thanks and a prayer of consecration of every affected part of the person's life back to the Lord. This offering of the parts of the body can be especially freeing when sexual sin has been involved. It is an application of offering ourselves to the Lord and thereby having the joy of knowing God's way is the best way for them in the future:

> 'Therefore, I urge you, brothers, in view of God's mercy, to offer your bodies as living sacrifices, holy and pleasing to God – this is your spiritual act of worship. Do not conform any longer to the pattern of this world, but be transformed by the renewing of your mind. Then you will be able to test and approve what God's will is – his good, pleasing and perfect will.' (Rom. 12:1–2)

Helping Someone Release Forgiveness

When we have been sinned against and are traumatised by that experience it is very easy to build resentment, anger and unforgiveness towards the person who has done this. We can become so tormented by it that every area of our lives is affected and we become the victim of the enemy.

Forgiveness means that we stop feeling resentment against someone who has hurt us and we cancel a person's record with us and transfer the responsibility for any punishment to God.

In ministering this freedom we may need to gently point out why it is so necessary to forgive:

- Because in Christ God forgave us and restored our relationship with Him (Eph. 4:32).
- Because unless we forgive we will struggle to experience forgiveness ourselves (Matt. 6:15).
- Because forgiveness releases us from the past, restores the present and heals us for the future.
- Because forgiveness enables us to empty our hearts of hatred.
- Because forgiveness opens us to Christ's power to be healed.

In prayer we need to take a person through a number of steps. The order here is often significant, as it is sometimes tempting to jump too quickly ahead before the person is ready to take that step. Be patient in leading someone down this road:

1. Ask God by His Holy Spirit to show you together the root cause of the hurt.
2. Allow the person to describe the trauma and then to express to God the pain of the hurt – this may involve them reliving the moment and involve strong emotion, including crying, wailing or anger.
3. When they are ready, ask the person to resolve and be willing to forgive the perpetrator for the action and the attitude that caused the hurt.
4. Bring them to the point where they can ask God to forgive the perpetrator for causing the hurt. Sometimes it is not possible to move from point 3 to 4 in one prayer session. It may take some time – weeks or even months – before they are able to ask God to forgive rather than judge the person. Don't push a

person to do this before they are ready – the Holy Spirit will bring the willing person to this point at some stage.

5. Now ask them to ask God to forgive them for their own sins of bitterness, anger, resentment etc, that they have held on to.

6. Get them to bless aloud the perpetrator by name and encourage them to do that silently whenever they think of the perpetrator again, even in their absence.

7. Ask the Holy Spirit to come, to heal the hurt, and to fill them with new hope for a life free from unforgiveness and its consequences.

This process is one that we can lead a person through even if the perpetrator is dead. The point about unforgiveness is that it binds and harms the person unwilling to forgive, not the perpetrator. Not even the death of the perpetrator will release the hurting person.

Ministering forgiveness is the kingdom ministry that Jesus intends His Church to have:

> 'I will give you the keys of the kingdom of heaven; whatever you bind on earth will be bound in heaven, and whatever you loose on earth will be loosed in heaven.'
> (Matt. 16:19)

It is effectively setting people free from all the guilt, shame, and self-blame that sin brings in its wake. When this happens in our spirits every aspect of life is changed; it is as if the burdens are lifted and we are free to 'walk on air'.

The significance of this ministry is shown by the fact that Jesus explicitly commissions His disciples to do this in one of His post-resurrection encounters with them:

'"As the Father has sent me, I am sending you." And with that he breathed on them and said, "Receive the Holy Spirit. If you forgive anyone his sins, they are forgiven; if you do not forgive them, they are not forgiven."' (John 20:21–23)

Jesus is speaking both about the power of what He has achieved on the cross and the significance of Christians engaging in this ministry. Only through His death can God's forgiveness be received, and only if Christians communicate this message and ministry can it be experienced. And for this ministry to be powerfully effective Jesus has to breathe His Spirit on His disciples. In the light of these words it is noteworthy that in churches where there is an emphasis on the supernatural work of the Spirit there is normally a similar emphasis on the ministry of forgiveness. The first leads naturally to the second.

The more I go on in life the more aware I become of people with unresolved issues in their lives which are destroying them. They are looking for a type of acceptance which will give them a change in their self-image and enable them to make a new start. Only Jesus can do that. In ministering forgiveness we need to remain unshockable, patient and merciful. The guile and the depravity of the enemy know no bounds, and we will find ourselves needing to listen and respond with great grace to those who have become victims of the enemy in this way.

11

Filling With the Spirit

During the course of our ministry, we will often be ministering to Christians who want to be filled afresh with the Holy Spirit out of a desire to deepen their relationship with the Father. When a person asks for this, first talk it over with them and try to discover if there are any obvious barriers that might prevent them from experiencing the fullness of the Holy Spirit. Below I have listed several common obstructions that can keep people from having this experience.

Possible Barriers

Ignorance

It is possible that the person has a vague theological knowledge of the Holy Spirit, but has not grasped the fact that He is willing and able to fill and irradiate their lives with assurance, joy, peace in believing, and power to live and be a witness for Jesus. This is a bit like the people of Ephesus who replied, when Paul asked if they had received the Holy Spirit, '*We have not ever heard that there is a Holy Spirit"* (Acts 19:2). So many people long for peace, joy and a deep sense of assurance, but miss the fact that it is the filling of the Spirit that leads them into this full appreciation of their birthright as Christians.

When ministering to the person, speak about God's longing to give His Holy Spirit to all who ask. Then read and explain the following Bible passages to them:

> 'And afterward, I will pour out my Spirit on all people. Your **sons** and **daughters** will prophesy, your **old** men will dream dreams, your **young** men will see visions. Even on my servants, both **men and women**, I will pour out my Spirit in those days.' (Joel 2:28–9)

> 'Peter replied, "Repent and be baptized, every one of you, in the name of Jesus Christ for the forgiveness of your sins. And you will receive the gift of the Holy Spirit. The promise is for you and your children and for all who are far off – for **all** whom the Lord our God will call."' (Acts 2:38–39)

> 'If you then, though you are evil, know how to give good gifts to your children, how much more will your Father in heaven give the Holy Spirit **to those who ask him!**' (Luke 11:13)

The emphasis added to the verses above highlight their common theme – that of God's willingness to give to all who ask, whatever their age, sex or background.

Hostility and fear

Sometimes people have not experienced the fullness of God's presence out of a fear of surrendering and becoming vulnerable to Him. This usually stems from a person's negative experiences of authority figures. If a person has been treated badly or had bad experiences with those in authority over them in the past, it is common for them to transfer these experiences onto God and consequently they become uncertain or uncomfortable at the thought of a close relationship with Him. It is quite common to find real fear, not just reticence, over what God might do to the person if they were to open themselves completely to the Holy Spirit, become intimate with Him, and let Him be Lord over every aspect of their life.

If this is the case, reassure the person of the unconditional nature of God's love. Read and explain appropriate Scriptures, such as,

> 'We know and rely on the love God has for us. God is love.' (1 John 4:16)

> '"For I know the plans I have for you," declares the LORD, "plans to prosper you and not to harm you, plans to give you hope and a future."' (Jer. 29:11)

See also 1 John 4:9–21.

Spiritual and moral barriers

Sometimes in larger gatherings, such as conferences, people will come forward and ask to be filled with the Spirit before they have really made a commitment to Christ. In this scenario, sensitively enquire whether they have done so, and if not, take them through the prayer of commitment outlined in Chapter 9.

Similarly, if you discern that the person may be holding unforgiveness in their heart, encourage them to pray about the issue with you and help them to release forgiveness along the lines of the previous chapter. Be aware, however, that sometimes a fresh filling with the love of God by the Spirit helps someone to release and/or receive true forgiveness.

Another barrier can come in the form of dubious 'spiritual' involvement that the person has previously been involved in. Often those who are seeking spiritual truth, but who are misguided in their approach, can try various other methods before turning to Christ. To them these things may have seemed fairly harmless, but the Bible describes them as the 'occult'. Such things may have included consultations with fortune tellers, palm readers, Ouija boards, horoscopes, etc. As innocuous as some of these seem to many, they are in fact spiritually dangerous and damaging and can lead to a great spiritual oppression in someone's life. This is why God warns us:

> 'Let no one be found among you . . . who practices divination or sorcery, interprets omens, engages in witchcraft . . .' (Deut. 18:10)

There may be a moral barrier preventing a person from experiencing all God has for them. They may, for instance, have been living in an immoral relationship or engaging in immoral practises of one sort or another. If this is the case, they will need to confess their sin, repent and receive forgiveness from God.

Finally, though a person really wants to experience all that God has for them, they may be struggling with unbelief. This could be the result of erroneous teaching they have received in the past, informing them that God doesn't empower people in such a way any more. Or, they may simply struggle to believe God really wants to bless them in this way. If this is the case, tell them that there is no shame in confessing our unbelief to God and asking for His help to overcome it. God is not so offended by our unbelief that He is unable or unwilling to respond to our cries for help. What He seems to respond to is the cry of the needy, even when the cry of faith is mixed with uncertainty or unbelief. When a father brought his epileptic son to the disciples and they failed to heal him he must have been disappointed and wondered whether his son would ever be healed. When Jesus arrives on the scene and finds out what is going on the father says:

'I do believe; help me overcome my unbelief!' (Mark 9:24)

I believe that it's this sort of honest throwing ourselves at the feet of Jesus that He loves responding to. So encourage someone in this position of uncertainty to pray a similar prayer.

Being Filled With the Holy Spirit

Below is an outline of how you might lead someone through the process of being filled with the Holy Spirit.

Preparation

Depending on the circumstances, this could involve:

- Confession of sin.
- Renouncing any involvement in demonic activity.
- Forgiving those who have been hurtful.
- Renouncing a wrong relationship.

It may be necessary at this stage to speak forgiveness in Jesus' name and/or cut the person free in areas of bondage through Jesus' name.

Explain that the Holy Spirit does not come without His gifts and ask the person if they want and are willing to be released into the gifts of the Spirit, even the gift of tongues. This is an obviously supernatural gift and some are frightened of receiving it. To want to receive it is one sign of a willingness to make the Holy Spirit the Lord of their whole life, rather than just a visitor in the guest room. To be unwilling to receive this gift can be a sign of an unwillingness to be really filled to overflowing with the Spirit.

Explain about how wonderful the gift of tongues is for everyone who wants to be drawn closer to God in prayer and be built up in their faith:

> 'A person who speaks in a tongue speaks not to men but to God . . . he utters mysteries in the Spirit . . . He who speaks in a tongue edifies himself.' (1 Cor. 14:1–4)

Having said this, we know that many who have been filled with the Holy Spirit have not yet spoken in tongues, even though we believe that they could easily do so.

Just as wanting to receive and use the gifts of the Spirit indicates a readiness to be filled afresh, so too does a desire to be an effective witness for Jesus. This is the context in which Jesus promised the power of the Spirit to the first disciples:

> 'But you will receive power when the Holy Spirit comes on you; and you will be my witnesses in Jerusalem, and in all Judea and Samaria, and to the ends of the earth.' (Acts 1:8)

So a good question to ask as we prepare to pray for a person is 'Are you willing and wanting to live your life as a witness for Jesus, telling people anywhere and everywhere about how much he loves them and has done for them?' A positive answer to that question will normally also be accompanied by a realisation of inability to do it without the indwelling power of the Spirit.

This was certainly true for me. I had been a Vicar for about 18 months and was acutely aware of my impotence in bringing people to faith in Jesus. It was in desperation and longing that I began to pray 'Lord I need to be filled afresh with your Spirit to bring people to know you'. In his mercy God heard my cry and there began a new adventure in discovering the limitless nature of God's mercy and power.

Receiving the filling

This may take a little time. It is not a case of waving a magic wand! It is a case of giving God time to fill one of His children with an overwhelming and overflowing awareness of His presence, His love, His peace and His power. Therefore this is not an event to be rushed, but to be celebrated and enjoyed.

Encourage the person to ask for Jesus to fill them with His Spirit. Lay hands on them in an appropriate way and pray quietly for Jesus to fill them with His Spirit, at the same time inviting the person to be open and welcome Him.

Be sensitive to any prophetic words the Spirit gives you for the person being prayed for. This can build up faith and help people to open up further to the filling of the Spirit.

Watch for manifestations of the Spirit's presence and bless all that He is doing. Get them to express their thanks to Jesus for filling them with His Spirit and for what He is doing in their life right now.

Ask the person whether they would like to speak in tongues. Explain that, at first, it will often seem as if they are making it up and will not feel so much like a 'language' as strange sounds. Explain that any young child learns language in this way before moving on to form a vocabulary, syntax and grammar over a period of time.

Now pray quietly alongside them in tongues and ask God to release this gift in them. If necessary, pray for God to release their throat, their mouth and their tongue. And maybe with a hand on their stomach pray for God to release *'streams of living water . . . from within him'* (John 7:38).

Encourage them to 'have a go', and as they begin to speak in their new language, encourage them that this really is God's gift to them. Sometimes it can help to suggest that the person actually copies the sounds that you are making as you pray (slowly and quietly aloud) in tongues. This can often be the trigger to release a person from feeling their mind always has to be in control of and fully understand the sound of the words coming out their mouth. Although this may sound like 'cheating' at tongues it has parallels in the way that many people learn to speak a foreign language. Don't you remember having to repeat the sounds of, say, French as your teacher tried to teach you a new verb? You did it in the end because they assured you it would make sense to the French even if it made no sense to you! It's the same with the gift of tongues: it won't make sense to us, because it is another language, but it will make sense to God. Someone learning to speak in tongues will often need encouragement to know that their 'sound' is a legitimate language. After the first few syllables of copying you the person you have released will normally quickly gain confidence and start praying their own words in another language.

Of course, experiences vary enormously. There have been occasions when we have prayed for people to be filled with the Spirit and almost before we have got the words out of our mouths they have immediately started praying aloud in tongues. It is as if a tap has been turned on and the praise and thanks to God that they have bottled up inside them for years has been released. On the other hand, some need to be coached more closely. I remember trying to release someone in tongues who was a great linguist – she could speak three languages fluently and was learning another two. After praying for a while she said she could not speak in tongues unless she knew not only the words of that language but also the syntax and the grammar! I wasn't sure what to do so I said, 'I will pray aloud in my tongue and if you want to join in or copy what I am saying you can.' I only got the first word out before she said, 'Stop! What was that word?' I repeated it only to be told by her that it was the very word in her mind that she was too afraid to speak out aloud because she thought she was making it up. That's the fear of many when praying for people to be released in tongues, we need to develop ways of helping them to overcome this fear.

Afterwards we should give people the opportunity to ask questions about what has just happened. If there have been any prophetic words, write them down and encourage them to pray over them in the days ahead. Encourage the use of tongues daily in their personal prayer time. Remind them the gift is theirs to use, or not, whenever they choose to pray like that:

> 'So what shall I do? I will pray with my spirit, but I will also pray with my mind; I will sing with my spirit, but I will also sing with my mind.' (1 Cor. 14:15)

Tell them they can also use the gift during sung worship in public meetings. This can be a good place to 'practise' and get familiar with the sound of one's own voice speaking another language. Remind them the enemy does not want to see God's children being equipped with the power tools of the Holy Spirit with which to oppose him, and will be tempting the recent recipient to give up, insinuating, 'it's all rubbish'.

Seeing someone filled to overflowing with God's Spirit is a joyous and rewarding experience. Look for opportunities to help people experience the fullness of all that Christ has for them whenever you minister to others.

12

Ministering Deliverance

The ministry of deliverance or, to put it another way –
the healing of the oppressed – is a normal part of
Christ's commission to all His disciples (Luke 9:1).
Deliverance, therefore, is an integral part of Christian
ministry to individuals today. There has been much
written (and in my view speculated) about 'deliverance
ministry' and while much of this has been well-inten-
tioned, often it has added an unnecessary intrigue and
mystery to this area of ministry. We have no need to be
frightened of or even impressed by demons. We serve
the Lord of the Universe, to whom *all power and authority in heaven and on earth has been given* (Matt. 28:18), so
there is never any question about who is stronger. In
addition, we can rest assured of Christ's protection
when we are involved in this ministry because,

> 'The one who is in you is greater than the one who is in
> the world.' (1 John 4:4)

What are Demons?

Demons are evil spirits, agents of the enemy, who seek to trouble and destroy some aspect of our life or personality. The authorised version of the Bible often refers to them as 'unclean'. In Jesus' ministry we see Him dealing with demons which have brought sickness, such as blindness, dumbness, or epilepsy, and who manifest aggressively.

Jesus did not develop a demonology, though He does reveal to us quite a lot about the devil himself. It is clear from the rest of the New Testament that there are a variety of evil forces under a unified head, the devil himself. Jesus' main concern was to cast out demons from those afflicted by them, so that they could enjoy life as God intends it to be. Our main concern ought to be the same, rather than the building of a speculative demonology, based on minimal biblical evidence.

In the gospels there are clearly different degrees of oppression. Some are described simply as, '*Those troubled by evil spirits*' (Luke 6:18), and after prayer they were healed. Others are more clearly possessed, as in the case of the man who lived in the graveyard (Mark 5). Generally, because of the stigma attached to this, it is more helpful to talk about being 'demonised' than demon-possessed. 'Demonised' can be used in the same way we use the word 'sick'. If we describe someone as 'sick' it may mean anything ranging from a headache to a long-term, life threatening illness. So 'demonised' could mean, at one end of the spectrum, that a person struggles with powerful temptations on a frequent basis which they recognise to be assaults of the enemy, but which they are able to resist; or even that a demon has a major stronghold in their life such that they are dysfunctional in some part of their life. But, at the other end of the spectrum, it could mean that a person is physically and socially in a place of complete breakdown. It seems as if some of the people Jesus ministered to were in this state of complete breakdown:

> 'A man with an evil spirit came from the tombs to meet him. This man lived in the tombs, and no-one could bind him any more, not even with a chain. For he had often been chained hand and foot, but he tore the chains apart and broke the irons on his feet. No-one was strong enough to subdue him. Night and day among the tombs and in the hills he would cry out and cut himself with stones.' (Mark 5:2–5)

How Do They Gain Access?

Demons can gain access whenever people are in some way involved in spiritual rebellion against God. This is what the devil did when as an angel, created by God, he became proud and rebelled. He involved other angels in that rebellion, who are now his demons. When the human race fell, through temptation by the devil, the human race became involved in that rebellion. When individual human beings become deliberately rebellious against God today they open themselves up to demonisation.

There are a number of common entry points or footholds:

• Deliberate sin and uncontrolled emotions. *'In your anger do not sin; do not let the sun go down while you are still angry, and do not give the devil a foothold'* (Eph. 4:26–7). Uncontrolled anger is not the only type of habitual sin that gives the devil a foothold.

Alcoholism, drug abuse, hatred, violence, abuse of power and privilege are others. Emotional traumas, strong negative attitudes resulting from past hurts or deprivations, and wilful unforgiveness are also commonly used by the devil to bring his oppression into people's lives.

- Sexual immorality. '*Flee from sexual immorality. All other sins a man commits are outside his body, but he who sins sexually sins against his own body. Do you not know that your body is a temple of the Holy Spirit, who is in you, whom you have received from God? You are not your own*' (1 Cor. 6:18–19). Here Paul is suggesting that if we are involved in sexual immorality we are opening our bodies up to be the 'temple' for other spirits rather than the Holy Spirit.

- False worship of other gods. '*You belong to your father, the devil, and you want to carry out your father's desire . . . When he lies, he speaks his native language, for he is a liar and the father of lies*' (John 8:44). Involvement in any kind of worship which steadfastly denies that Jesus is the Christ, and especially occult practices, séances, Ouija boards, witchcraft and the like open people up to a control from the enemy because they are based on the ultimate lie: namely that Jesus is not the unique Son through whom alone we can both approach God and be restored to a relationship with Him.

- Generational sin. '*You shall not bow down to them or worship them; for I, the LORD your God, am a jealous God, punishing the children for the sin of the fathers to the third and fourth generation of those who hate me*' (Ex. 20:5). Sometimes people become oppressed by demonic forces as a result of the sin of their parents or ancestors, possibly as the result of a covenant with the devil entered into on their part by a

parent or guardian or due to some other generational sin.

One Saturday when I was on the streets with our healing team, I gave a leaflet to a woman and offered to pray
for her as she left Waitrose and walked along the pave-
ment. She (like most) looked somewhat surprised, but I
persevered saying that we were from a local church and
wanted to bless people with God's healing love. 'Is there
anything we can pray for you?' I repeated. 'No, but
please pray for my partner who is not sleeping,' she
replied. We found out his name and a few more details
and then prayed for him. She began to weep and then
said, 'So many things have gone wrong in my life, I feel
as if I've been plagued by bad luck.' (It's interesting how
many people begin by asking us to pray for a friend or
relative who is not present, and then when they realise
we pray with compassion and empathy ask us to pray
something for them too! It's as if they are testing us out
before trusting us with something personal).

I was prompted to ask, 'When did that start? Did anything particular happen to provoke that feeling?' 'Yes,'
she replied. 'It started when I was 18 and I am now in
my fifties.' I was shocked by her immediate openness
and clarity and my heart went out to her as I thought of
her struggling with life for over 30 years. She explained
that she had been stalked by a man in a car on a couple
of occasions and then one day he had shouted to her
through his open car window as he drove alongside her,
'If you don't come with me I will curse you with bad
luck for the rest of your life.' She had never told anyone
of this traumatic event and I believe this had given the
enemy a way of assaulting her all her life until that
point. Needless to say we prayed for her deliverance,
breaking the power of this undeserved curse (Proverbs

26:2) and setting her free in the name of Jesus. She left us saying, 'Something has left me . . . a burden has been lifted' and 'I haven't felt like this for more than 30 years!'

Indications of an Evil Spirit's Presence

There are a number of ways in which we can discern the presence of a demonic spirit. This is an important gift to ask for and to develop both because demons will try to hide themselves from the presence of Jesus, and also because some will come for prayer saying, 'I think I have a demon' when they haven't at all!

- Revelation from the Holy Spirit. This needs careful checking – it is unwise ever to suggest to someone they are demonised. In the end demons will normally reveal themselves through other 'symptoms'.
- Manifestations in reaction to a power 'encounter' in worship or when the Spirit comes in power in a meeting. Often demons will produce a convulsive reaction in a person in response to the presence of the Spirit of God as He comes to deliver. But great care and discernment is needed because people can also respond to the anointing of God with strange manifestations.
- When being prayed for there may be:
  - ♦ A more violent physical response to the name of Jesus or the phrase 'the blood of the cross.'
  - ♦ Pain moving about in the person's body or eyes rolling back in their sockets.
  - ♦ A 'spirit' speaking within so that the person is hearing voices.
  - ♦ A 'different' voice speaking out aloud through the person.

♦ Disengagement from the ministry with sleepiness, inertness, or 'deathlike' symptoms.

One way to discern whether a spirit is present is to begin a prayer such as, 'I shine the light of Jesus into any dark places in your life' or 'I bring you to the foot of the cross where Jesus shed His blood for you.' Then wait and see how the person responds as the Holy Spirit takes your words into the person's spirit.

- A dread of going into any place with a strong Christian association (i.e. a church), or shouting out in worship, or blaspheming at the mention of the name of Jesus, or the blood of Jesus shed on the cross.
- Yielding to compulsive desires which are clearly out of control, including self-mutilation, self-destructive tendencies and having active destructive and aggressive attitudes towards others.

Some of the 'apparent symptoms' of oppression could be signs of the Holy Spirit touching deep hurts and not necessarily evidence of demonic activity at all. Additionally an anointing for prophecy or intercession can also be accompanied by strange contortions and noise, so great care is needed in discernment.

Guidelines for Ministry

- If during general ministry you come across the need for deliverance you can often do this relatively silently and quickly. However, should there be no adequate conclusion to the ministry it is best, in consultation with the church leadership, to deliberately plan a convenient time for further ministry. It is not always necessary to deal with the issue immediately.

- Be careful about choosing the time for ministry. A suitable appointment during daylight is often better than dealing with this late at night. Make sure it is at a time when others can join you – it is unwise to minister on your own.
- Prepare yourself before a planned ministry time. Confess any sins, seek a fresh anointing of the Holy Spirit and put on the whole armour of God. Sometimes a time of prayer and fasting beforehand can speed up deliverance.
- Check whether the individual is under medical supervision, medication or has a history of mental illness. Demonic oppression may not be the most serious problem the person has – long-term traumatised emotions may be more problematic. If so, it is important that deliverance ministry should be part of the healing process that has already begun, rather than overrule or arrest this.
- It is unwise ever to suggest to someone that they have an evil spirit until you have checked it out with others in the church's leadership. When you are reasonably sure this is the case, minister in mixed groups of three or four for any significant ministry, and with at least one of the same sex present. Do not allow bystanders to congregate – the devil loves drawing attention to his work. Jesus sometimes drew people aside to minister privately to them.
- Encourage the person to be relaxed and to focus on Jesus. Invite the Holy Spirit to come and then listen to the Lord and 'track' what the Spirit is doing. Remember that at any time in the course of ministry you can stop and talk. The agreement and cooperation of the person is usually vital. They will also often be able to discern and talk about what is happening inside them. Sometimes people fail to cooperate

because they sense the demon's fear and think it's their own, or they feel they will lose something of their identity if the demon were to leave.

- Treat the person the way you would like to be treated yourself if you were the one being ministered to. Offer any words of knowledge sensitively. Always remember you could be wrong. Similarly try to find words which do not imply guilt.

- Tell the person that during the ministry you will sometimes be addressing the spirit directly and sometimes be talking to them. Assure them of God's infinite love for them, His hatred of the enemy and all that the enemy has done to them, and His ability and longing to free them.

- Don't allow excessive manifestations. Rebuke or bind the evil spirit in the name of Jesus. If the demon is apparently in total control (sometimes with the help of drink or drugs) and you are unable to get through to the real person, then do not persist in ministry. Let the afflicted person sleep it off and return to the ministry at a suitable date later.

- It is sometimes taught that you need to know the demon's name. It might be revealed in the process of dialogue. Although this is supposed to be a help, the demon itself is not likely to give its own name away readily and even if it did it could not be trusted anyway because demons come from the father of lies! It is best to dialogue as little as possible with demons. Jesus frequently commanded them to 'be quiet' (Mark 1:25).

- Do demons come in clusters? This is often taught, but should never be assumed. It is best to allow plenty of time after the expulsion of a demon. An afflicted person (usually very keen to get delivered) may well continue to exhibit symptoms of demonisation if they think you believe there are still others there. We are all very susceptible to suggestion.

- The person receiving ministry needs to take responsibility and deal with their own sin, repenting where necessary and as the Spirit leads. Similarly, hurts, traumas and anything inherited needs to be acknowledged and renounced, asking for God's help where needed. Often oppression lifts at this stage even without formal 'expulsion'.

- At an appropriate moment, address the demon directly in Jesus' name and command it to go. Looking straight into the eyes of the person whilst doing this can help. Advise the person to cooperate fully by putting their will into this. There is no point in continuing if the person will not cooperate in this way.

- If there is no response to a firm command, ask the Holy Spirit for guidance. Remember it's the power of God which shifts demons, not you, so shouting won't help! If in doubt or you come to a blockage, delay rather than labour on.

- Check with the person whether the oppression seems to have gone. They will normally be aware of an inner struggle during deliverance and will know when they are freed.

- Once the person is delivered, pray for their infilling with the Holy Spirit and give glory to God.

- Always finish by praying for the peace of God to fill them.

Follow Up

We need to recognise that any person freed from demonic oppression will need ongoing support. We can encourage the person to contact us again if necessary. In any case, it is a helpful practice to try to contact them within the next forty-eight hours if at all possible, to ask how they are. Sometimes people are left physically, emotionally and spiritually exhausted in the immediate aftermath of deliverance. They may need to rest and relax to recover. Their continuing healing from the trauma of what the enemy has done to them will come as they learn to stand in their healing. This will include worshipping God in Spirit and truth, receiving communion, enjoying being a part of the healing community which the Church is meant to be, and belonging to a small accountability group like a home group.

13

Pastoral Prayer Ministry

Pastoral Prayer Ministry (PPM), sometimes referred to as 'inner healing' is an ongoing ministry to deeper needs that people have, often of an emotional and psychological nature. Almost as soon as healing prayer ministry is offered in most churches it is apparent that some people's needs have not been adequately addressed during after-service prayer ministry. Some provision for dealing with these needs on a planned basis over a longer period of time is helpful if the local church is to become the healing community that God really intends it to be. A team will need to trained and deployed under a wisely appointed, and suitably equipped, team leader.

Levels of Need

Our churches are full of people with little understanding about where their own responsibility lies for their healing and growth. This is where other Christians, empowered by the Spirit, can help them. God has placed us in the community of the Church precisely so that we can help each other to grow to maturity.

'Carry each other's burdens, and in this way you will fulfil the law of Christ.' (Gal. 6:2)

At the same time we should learn to stand on our own two feet:

'Each one should carry his own load.' (Gal. 6:5)

In a healthy church many people will find measures of healing from all sorts of emotional traumas as they engage in Spirit-filled worship, as they seek the Lord through the Scriptures, and as they avail themselves of the victory of Jesus on the cross. But another God-given way of receiving healing is through the prayer of fellow believers:

'Therefore confess your sins to each other and pray for each other so that you may be healed.' (Jas. 5:16)

Some of this confession, prayer and healing should be happening during the regular after-service prayer ministry. This may occur on a one-off occasion or over a period of weeks, during which time an individual seeks prayer weekly. Some of it may also be happening in an effective, holistic small group, in which people can be open and honest about their lives and receive prayer ministry.

However, there are some who have experienced deep hurt and emotional trauma, often as a result of dysfunctional family backgrounds, who need longer term help. Similarly, there are others who have made such wrong choices and fallen into sin so deeply, that they are now trapped in irrational beliefs and behaviour patterns which are destroying their lives. These people too may need longer term prayer ministry.

We recommend that this PPM is only offered to members of the church who are involved in its wider life though worship, prayer, teaching, serving and fellowship. These things help a person to continue to receive healing through a variety of means rather than simply ministry appointments.

In our own church we launched a PPM initiative called Oasis. People are invited into this programme after an initial assessment and then they join a small prayer group of maybe three people who will meet together regularly under the facilitation of two trained leaders. In this group we endeavour to bring together people with similar needs or facing similar issues and this has been the key to its success. Because ministry takes place in a small group, people have to want to be healed by God sufficiently to overcome the desire to have one-on-one attention. There is also a safeguard in having more than one person in the group, because it helps each person to genuinely seek God for their needs and not become dependent on a 'counsellor' or simply rely on input from the trained leader. This ultimately results in people developing both a sense of personal responsibility for their healing, and an accountability to others who are in the same process of healing. Some of the most effective ministers in our church today are people who were the most broken, but who were touched, healed and restored by God as they went through the course.

Guidelines

As always, it is helpful to engage in such ministry according to guidelines sanctioned by the church leadership. These are the kind of steps that need to be put in place if the church is to offer to help people in this way:

- This sort of ministry requires a certain amount of experience and time. A church needs to know whether it has people who have the necessary wisdom and experience and who are willing to give time to this ministry. Good training can complement experience, but this involves time too! It helps if everyone in this ministry is involved in the after-service ministry where they can regularly see God at work through His Holy Spirit.
- Some sort of 'assessing' process needs to be put in place by someone who is able to discern whether the person seeking help comes within the scope of the abilities of the PPM team. Knowing our limitations as well as the power of the Lord to heal is important if we are to exercise this ministry well.
- As with all other types of ministry it should not be undertaken alone, but in pairs, always using someone of the same sex as the individual coming for ministry. There should be a deep spiritual harmony between those ministering and, because this involves working very closely together, I would not recommend anyone to work in partnership with someone of the opposite sex apart from their spouse. Interestingly, we find that the better the relationship is between the pair the more effective and fruitful is the ministry. It's as if God has wired us to be at our best when we are working in real harmony with someone else; perhaps it's because we are then at our most relaxed and therefore at our most receptive to the promptings of the Spirit. This also makes a difficult and intense sort of ministry much more enjoyable!
- From experience I recommend an initial commitment to 4–6 sessions. After these have taken place the person's wholeness and spiritual wellbeing should be

reviewed before any further commitment is offered. This sort of time limitation is helpful because it encourages a person to focus their energy on making progress during the period, rather than leaving things open ended. It gives both sides a chance to review the effectiveness of the ministry and those ministering the opportunity to stop the ministry if they feel it is not being profitable.

- The availability of a prayer room within the church building is to be preferred over the use of the home. This helps both those ministering and the one receiving ministry to conduct this PPM in a planned and relatively business-like manner. It is important to maintain some necessary boundaries and to avoid any possible over-dependency developing. A session should be limited in length, normally to 90 minutes maximum, since they can be emotionally, spiritually and sometimes physically draining for everyone.

- The willingness and cooperation of the person seeking prayer is vital. Apart from cooperating during the ministry time, they may need to engage in the keeping of a 'prayer journal', the reading of prescribed scriptures and recommended Christian books, as well as the setting of some other interim goals to speed their healing. Outlining this clearly creates greater commitment to the exercise. In some cases, when ministry is difficult and there is no quick and easy resolution then reference back to this commitment can break the logjam.

- Brief notes should be maintained by the prayer couple. They should not be held centrally or copied and they must be kept absolutely confidential. The keeping of notes enables everyone to see what issues have been dealt with and what progress has been made.

- We should always value professional help and be quite willing to advise an individual to seek professional support when this is needed. If there is any doubt, with the individual's permission and the church leader's approval, the individual's doctor can be consulted. If the person is on medication this is especially important before engaging in prolonged PPM.

- If there is a local Christian doctor or psychiatrist available, they could be enlisted to act as a long-stop or reference point for the church or PPM team leader. This can create a degree of safety both for those seeking and those giving ministry.

God is all powerful. We have seen him do wonderful work in bringing healing to all sorts of traumatised people through the prayers of Christians who are open to the guidance and power of the Holy Spirit. However, it is not possible to learn to run before trying to walk, so we need to realise that initiating, establishing and then developing a PPM will be a long term commitment that requires wisdom, energy and perseverance. Keeping in close touch with other churches on the same learning curve can prove really helpful.

Part 4

Arenas of Ministry

14

In the Local Church

The natural place for healing ministry to take place is in and through the local church congregation. God gives gifts of healing from the Holy Spirit because He intends the people of God to become known as a healing community. This book is founded on this assumption. It is up to every church leader to determine to follow the lead of the Spirit and courageously establish a healing ministry in their church. Some 'religious' people may oppose this – they did in Jesus' day and He told us that we were to expect the same response from some.

> 'It is enough for the student to be like his teacher, and the servant like his master. If the head of the house has been called Beelzebub, how much more the members of his household!' (Matt. 10:25)

As we begin to introduce this ministry we may find, as David Pytches said, that 'It won't be long before they call your good evil.' Sadly some may reject the church's healing ministry and also question or even reject our leadership too (Matt. 10:14); but others will welcome it and then identify it as a genuine work of God. In an age of alternative medicine and of increasing openness to any type of spirituality which transcends the purely rational, many more are open to the influence of the supernatural than ever before.

The Church Leader's Role

If healing ministry is to have credibility and become effective in the life of a church, it must be 'owned' by the church leader. That person must believe in it, initiate it and take responsibility for seeing it develop. In practise they can not be closely involved in the prayer ministry, because this would draw them away from their other responsibilities and duties as the church leader, and it is a time consuming ministry, but the church leader can encourage this ministry and exercise leadership of it by . . .

Teaching

The whole church needs good biblically-based teaching on the need to face up to life's hurts, on how to receive God's healing for them, and on the work of the Holy Spirit in leading us into wholeness in Christ. This will bring a constant supply of people seeking this ministry. The whole healing team needs to be trained and supported, if not always by the leader directly, then by the provision of good training by others who share their values. Those involved in PPM will need additional and ongoing training, supervision and encouragement.

Delegation

Leaders may be in danger of falling into two traps. Firstly, they may over-delegate to the point of non-involvement, in which case the ministry will probably either die through lack of support or come into disrepute through lack of accountability. Secondly, the leader may become over-involved, resulting in over-control and a failure to empower others, resulting in them being frustrated at not being able to reach their full potential in exercising their God-given gifts.

Avoiding both of these traps requires a good understanding of delegation and accountability, both on the part of the church leader and on the part of the person appointed to lead the ministry team. Ideally they should have a natural and good relationship with each other, shared values for the way this particular ministry should be exercised in public services, and have a structured way of meeting and talking issues through on a relatively frequent basis. As in every area of ministry, people thrive on having more positive feedback than negative comments. For instance the question, 'What has the Lord been doing recently?' is always a springboard for eliciting testimonies. 'How can I support you better in this ministry?' will often lead to an honest revelation of any difficulties that the ministry team leader is experiencing. If the church leader has heard a story of someone who God has touched through the prayer team, start off by telling the team leader, 'I heard that Mrs Jones was healed last week.' The team leader will be thrilled that you are keeping your ear to the ground and have noticed what they are doing Sunday by Sunday! I recently read that the two main roles of a leader are to define reality and to say thank you. By introducing healing ministry into a church the leader is redefining the reality of God's desire and power to heal today just as He did when Jesus was physically present on Earth. By thanking the ministry team leader, the church leader is making them feel that their contribution to extending the kingdom of God is significant and worthwhile, even if at times tiring and difficult.

Creating a 'safe place'

Getting in touch with repressed emotions is never easy and people will not do it unless they feel they are in a 'safe place'. A lack of confidentiality, an obvious expression of shock over sin, or accusations of guilt are sure to make a church feel an *unsafe* place. A leader who is known and seen to be open, vulnerable, self-disclosing and in accountable relationships within the church can help to create a 'safe place' for others. This can be done both through teaching and example.

Authorisation

Those who are appointed to be the leaders of this ministry must carry the complete trust of the overall church leader, and at the same time be held in high regard by members of the church. This is an exposed position of high responsibility and those appointed should be known for their humility, purity and integrity as well as being full of faith and the Holy Spirit. They must be willing to exercise this ministry under the authority of the leader. The church leader must be happy with others who are appointed to the team and their decision must be allowed to overrule the opinion of the ministry team leader. The overall church leader is, in the end, accountable to God for the wise exercising of this ministry.

Resolving difficulties

Should there be any report or concern expressed by someone who has received inappropriate ministry in the church, the leader will need to deal with it straight away. They may choose to do this through the ministry team leader in the first instance, but ultimately they may have to get involved. If there is something definite to act on, then the team member may need to be placed again alongside someone more experienced and be reminded again of the values under-girding this ministry. In some cases a person may need to be asked to stand down for a while, especially if they are unwilling to receive discipline, or if they need to give attention to difficult issues in their own life. The way the church leader handles this kind of issue is important for the long term credibility of the ministry.

If this ministry is to flourish in a church then the leader *must* be involved to some degree. Most church leaders find it hard to permit things in their churches that they don't really believe in or feel 'at ease' with. This is because they have to give an account to God of their oversight of the church, and good leaders cannot take that lightly.

If you are reading this as a church member and your leader is not yet ready to introduce such a ministry publicly, there are a number of things you can do, whilst being careful not to operate in a maverick fashion or undermine your church leadership. First, take every opportunity you can to minister healing to people in your home and as you meet people in the normal course of your life. Second, continue to love and pray for your leaders and gently encourage them with stories of what God has been doing as you have ministered to people elsewhere. Third, try to take your leader with you to some appropriate event that will enable them to see God at work in a way which you think may help them to learn about it and accept it. Fourth, if they give you permission to develop something publicly as part of the church's ministry, always keep open and honest lines of communication with them and go at the pace they are allowing you to go, even if this is slower than you might like.

Introducing This Ministry

When Jesus sent out the disciples into the villages the advice He gave is equally appropriate for church leaders introducing this ministry today!

> 'I am sending you out like sheep among wolves. Therefore be as shrewd as snakes and as innocent as doves.' (Matt. 10:16)

Here are some helpful tips for church leaders wanting to introduce this ministry in their church, gleaned from others who have already done so:

- Commit yourself to ministering healing in this way on any and every occasion you can, both as you visit people in their homes and at the very end of services (once you have said goodbye to most people). Your example of involvement and the stories you will have to tell are indispensable in giving this ministry credibility and respectability in the church.
- Start to teach about this ministry from the Scriptures over a few weeks consecutively and ask people to give testimony to healings they have received in answer to prayer. These don't have to be spectacular –

they simply need to be from people that members of the church can relate to in such a way that they think, 'If that happened to them, it could happen to me.'

- If possible agree with your leadership team that this ministry is so important that it should be done in an orderly and effective way. In this way gain their permission and blessing. If they give it, they will help to build an environment of faith; if they resist this ministry in the long term, they may create an environment of doubt and scepticism which will hinder the miraculous as it did for Jesus in His home town.

- Train a ministry team (more detailed advice on this aspect is offered below). This training should be advertised publicly so that anyone can come, but it is important for the leader to recruit personally and privately to it anyone they really want to be involved. If you are not confident in preparing other material this book can be used as an outline for a training course. Alternatively, you can form a group to listen to teaching tapes together (helpful resources are available from www.new-wine.org). The teaching can be discussed together and then the group can pray for each other. New Wine is also happy to commend other church leaders who have been involved in this ministry for a while who can come and conduct a healing training day in your locality. We normally encourage a hosting church to invite other interested people and churches in their locality to join them for this training (see the end of this book for contact details).

- Decide when and where you are going to offer this ministry. Many churches now do so at the end of every main service. Also decide where in the building you will do this. Some like to have it in a side-chapel and some keep it highly visible at the front of the aisle. While the former offers anonymity, the latter keeps it as a publicly visible ministry. There are advantages and disadvantages in both, but try to do it in a place and way that enables people to see that this ministry is quite 'normal' and not 'special'.

- Appoint and authorise the team and a responsible team leader in a *public* service. The team leaders should be well respected by the congregation. It can help at such a public launch to have a visiting speaker whom you know to be committed to this ministry and who shares your values.
- Don't test the Lord. Sometimes in the early days of this ministry a highly visible member of the church becomes ill and they become a sort of 'test case' in the church to see if this ministry really works. We should never try to put God on trial in such a way. Apart from disobeying the command to not test God, it also violates the core value of 'love for the individual', treating them as some kind of guinea pig.
- From time to time invite a speaker and a ministry team from another church to your regular team training evening and/or to one of your church services or a special celebration. Knowing there will be a special emphasis on prayer for healing gives church members the extra courage to bring their sick friends and releases an extra degree of expectation and faith.
- Keep recruiting new people into the team, both by personal invitation and by offering training days or courses. If you offer healing prayer ministry at, or after, all your main services you will find that over a period of time God will start bringing people to your church who want to be healed and you will need a larger pool of people willing to spend time ministering healing to others.
- If possible, from time to time, get the whole church to minister to each other during a Sunday Service. This

ministry is for every Christian and not just for those 'on the ministry team'. Over time it is remarkably easy for the ministry team to become the only people involved in this ministry and to become a sort of 'closed shop'. If this is allowed to happen the full potential of this ministry will never be realised.

- Work with your small group leaders to ensure that they understand the vision and values that you have for this ministry and that they are allowing space and time for it in their small groups. A well run small group can offer a 'safe learning environment' where people can first learn to move in the gifts of the Spirit and start to minister healing. However, it is unwise to insist that every group must offer this ministry. It may be too threatening for some church members and we don't want to drive them away.
- Persevere. There may not be any spectacular healings for a while. When John Wimber pioneered this ministry in his church it was nine months before anyone experienced any measure of healing as a direct answer to their prayers. Fortunately, many churches have not had to wait this long before seeing the Lord bring healing through this ministry!

God rewarded our perseverance with this ministry as we began to see various people healed in various degrees. Initially some experienced partial healing, but healing nonetheless, whilst others were more dramatically healed. We had a lady called Jackie in our church who was fairly seriously deaf, with only 25% hearing in one ear. We prayed for her a number of times over many weeks, but all without any apparent improvement in her hearing level.

Then, Jackie attended a conference in America. At the end of one of the conference sessions there was an opportunity for people to be prayed for, so she went forward and received prayer. Once again there was no apparent or immediate improvement. However, she woke up later that night in her hotel room as she was disturbed by some noise. She recalls saying, 'This is a noisy hotel!' and was aware that she could hear a sound, though she wasn't sure what it was. Now fully awake, she realised the sound was that of the air conditioning unit in her room. Her hearing had been completely restored.

On another occasion, a member of our PCC hurt his back quite badly and was immobilised at home. I decided that I should visit him in his home and pray for him. I prayed that the Holy Spirit would come and touch and restore his back. There was no immediate or obvious change, but I sensed that 'something' had happened. I had stopped by before going to lead a small evangelistic meeting in a parishioner's house, so I told him that should he find he could get up and walk, he could drop by as an encouragement to everyone. I was expectant of him turning up, so I was somewhat disappointed when he didn't appear. However, a few days later I saw him walking around as normal and asked him what had happened.

The first thing he did was to apologise for not coming round to the house. After I had prayed for him, he had indeed felt different, so he tried getting up and found that he could move about without any pain. He was just thinking that he ought to come and tell me and the rest of the group about what God had done for him when his brother arrived to visit him, so he excitedly told his brother, rather than our group, all about it!

Healings such as these early on in the ministry gave us a great deal of encouragement that we should continue and not give up.

Selecting the Ministry Team

While we want to encourage every Christian to be involved in healing ministry we need to ensure that the ministry we offer people has an inherent quality and credibility. For this reason the leader must be wise and discerning in his selection of appropriate personnel for the ministry team and not just choose those people who are willing and available (though some of these may be the right people). It is the leader's job to both vet and authorise those involved.

For various reasons this ministry can sometimes attract people who are not yet ready to be involved. In training and appointing people we should look for those who are:

- Committed to following Jesus, evidenced both by a degree of understanding in their Christian faith and the fruit of the Spirit being seen in their lifestyle.
- Wanting to be continuously filled with the Holy Spirit and prayerfully seeking and using the gifts of the Spirit in ministry.
- On their own journey to wholeness and asking for healing ministry for themselves from time to time.
- Sensitive to people, reacting in acceptance and love, rather than shock and judgement, to the sins and traumas in which people so easily get trapped.
- Committed to the church fellowship and preferably part of one of the small groups – this indicates a real willingness to live in relationship with others.
- Willing to work under the authority of the church and ministry team leader and to adhere to the values, guidelines and practises that the church has adopted for public ministry.
- Reasonably 'respected' by and 'acceptable' to others in the church.

Sometimes those who are new to the faith and the church are the most teachable about this ministry, since they have no 'previous religious experience' which could have given them an alternative theology, value system or practice. So don't simply look to those who have been in the church for many years. At the same time, if there are some on the team who are 'stalwarts' of the church then this ministry can quickly gain credibility with others who have been around in the church for a long time, but for whom the idea of healing prayer ministry is initially quite strange or even threatening.

Exercising Ministry with Humility and Love

Above all, as with any ministry in the church, we need people leading it who are sensitive to the Holy Spirit and have an innate humility. This is very important when it comes to exercising the spiritual gifts in a public setting. Those who like the sound of their own voice or who are keen to show others how gifted they are will not be right for a healing ministry team. Team members should be able to minister to others with grace and be willing to be corrected at any point.

There are times when I have seen ministry teams assemble at the front of churches, when I have wondered whether I would be prepared to allow them to pray for me. I think to myself, 'If I was in need, would I go to these people?' There has to be a credibility but also an approachability about those who are to minister which gives people the confidence to come forward with their needs. No one is perfect, so we are not looking for perfect people, but they have to be those who have a sufficient understanding of God's grace that they won't judge people, but will listen and empathise, and can demonstrate the love of God to them.

In Philip Yancey's book *What's So Amazing About Grace?* he tells the story of a lady he spoke to and suggested she should try going to church. Her response was, 'Why would I want to go to church? I feel bad enough as it is!' Many outside the Church see it as being judgemental and critical, but this was not what Jesus was like and nor should we be. The outcasts of society who were rejected by the religious system of their day were attracted to Jesus because of His love for them. In fact, they couldn't keep away from Him! Though He didn't shy away from addressing the issue of sin in people's lives, He did so with an incredible love and compassion that people found compelling. Many more people will come to be ministered to if we exude the same attitude.

Confidentiality

Finally, confidentiality is an essential asset for any team member. Often the greatest fear of those in need is that once they confess their problems 'the news will be out'. Those coming for ministry will often have sensitive issues they need to discuss. The last thing they should be worried about is that the person ministering to them will immediately go and tell others.

Early on in my church leadership I had a small accountability group, the ground rules of which were that whatever was discussed stayed within the four walls of our meeting place. I once decided to be open and vulnerable about the fact that I found a small group of people in the church fairly overbearing and manipulative, which was making my job of leadership more difficult. I was horrified when, on the following Sunday, a member of this 'group' approached me and said, 'I'm so sorry you're finding us overbearing and manipulative!' I knew then that not everyone understood the ground rules of the accountability group!

If anything like this happened in the context of the prayer ministry team, it would very quickly erode the trust of those in need and the ministry would become ineffective. Character and discretion must be the hallmark of team members. When this is the case, many more broken people are attracted to come to God for healing.

15

Other Arenas of Ministry

In a Special Time of Outpouring of the Spirit

Over the last twenty years there have been some occasions when churches have experienced major visitations of the Holy Spirit, resulting in many people coming for prayer for general renewal and a refreshing of their walk with God. These times have often been accompanied by powerful manifestations, such as shaking, falling, laughing, weeping and loud cries.

During these times individuals go through powerful experiences of meeting with God. These often result in repentance over sin, a greater awareness of God's love, a deepening of their adoration for Jesus, in healing of life's hurts, and in anointing with power for new or renewed ministries. There is often a great sense of awe at being in the presence of a Holy God.

In such times, prayer ministry should be exercised using the same values as outlined earlier. But we must exercise an even greater sensitivity to what the Holy Spirit is doing. The following are some guidelines regarding how to pray for people in such a setting.

A very helpful opening prayer is: 'Father, I bless what you are doing in this person's life.' It is also helpful to be able to pray biblical prayers, such as these, as the Spirit leads:

- To be filled with the Spirit.
  'Be filled with the Spirit.' (Eph. 5:18)
- To know God better.
  '[I ask that] *God . . . may give you the Spirit of wisdom and revelation, so that you may know him better.'* (Eph. 1:17)
- To let the light overcome the darkness.
  'I pray also that the eyes of your heart may be enlightened.' (Eph. 1:18)
- To know even more of God's love.
  'I pray that you [may] grasp how wide and long and high and deep is the love of Christ.' (Eph. 3:17)
- To have renewed joy.
  'Restore . . . the joy of your salvation.' (Ps. 51:12)
- To have inner strength.
  'I pray that out of his glorious riches God may strengthen you with power through his Spirit in your inner being.' (Eph. 3:16)
- To know God's peace always.
  'May the Lord of peace himself give you peace at all times and in every way.' (2 Thess. 3:16)
- To live a holy life.
  'And we pray . . . that you may live a life worthy of the Lord and may please him in every way.' (Col. 1:10)
- To bring glory to Jesus.
  'We pray . . . that the name of our Lord Jesus may be glorified in you.' (2 Thess. 1:12)
- To know God's will and calling.
  'Your kingdom come, your will be done on earth as it is in heaven.' (Matt. 6:10)

- To be anointed in their calling.
  'The Holy Spirit said, "Set apart for me Barnabas and Saul for the work to which I have called them." So after they had fasted and prayed, they placed their hands on them and sent them off.' (Acts 13:2)
- To share their faith.
  'I pray that you may be active in sharing your faith.' (Phil. 1:6)
- To know God's protection.
  'My prayer is not that you take them out of the world but that you protect them from the evil one.' (John 17:15)
- For grace to persevere.
  'May the grace of the Lord Jesus Christ, and the love of God, and the fellowship of the Holy Spirit be with you.' (2 Cor. 13:14)

As in every other setting, the ministry is always helped by asking a question at some stage about what the Lord is doing or saying, and asking whether there is anything specific the person is seeking God for and for which you can pray. But in times of great outpouring of the Spirit many people are quite happy to 'soak' in the presence of God without specific prayer, and those ministering need to allow this to happen without constant interruption.

In a Conference Setting

All this prayer ministry is about cooperating with God. In a conference setting it's important also to cooperate with the person coordinating the ministry from the front. Learning to listen to their instructions as well as looking around and 'seeing what God is doing', while at the same time being sensitive to the prompting of the Spirit as you minister to an individual, is an art!

As in other settings, it is always good to minister in pairs, ensuring that there is at least one person of the same sex as the person you are ministering to. Also, take particular care in a crowd not to invade someone's 'space'.

- Be careful not to confuse a display of emotion with an evil spirit. It is better to begin ministry on the assumption that repressed hurt is being manifested. It is best not to tell a person they have an evil spirit, even if you think they have. Deliverance can often be done without any obvious 'naming' and 'shouting' at demons. They can be driven out simply by the presence and power of God, and a quiet word of command.
- Be sensitive to those who are quietly seeking God, rather than ministering only to those who are obviously manifesting 'noisily'. A large crowd can encourage those who are given to displays of emotion to attract attention to themselves in a way that diverts the ministry team from looking out for those who are hungrily seeking God in other ways. These less obvious people are equally important.
- Introduce yourself by name and discover the name of the person you are praying for if you don't know it already. Ask if you can pray for them. Being natural and friendly like this helps puts people at ease with you.
- Encourage anyone on whom you 'see the Spirit resting' to open themselves further to His work in them. Assure them that God is good and that all His plans and purposes are good for them. Some may be afraid of intimacy with God or of opening up to Him emotionally in front of others. Create a safe place around them and encourage them appropriately by saying things like, 'Don't be afraid . . . It's okay to express

your feelings ... You can stop at any time, but try to go with it' etc.

- Remember, people need to take responsibility for their own life and response to God. Wherever possible get them to pray out aloud for what they are seeking. This ensures they are not just expecting us to 'wave a magic wand' over them so that everything will get better. As the ministry progresses their own involvement in discerning what God is doing is important. They have even more responsibility to hear from the Lord than do those ministering.

- Don't let people become dependent on you by promising that you will pray for them personally at the next meeting of the conference. Assure them that this is God's work and that He can continue through the times of worship and teaching, as well as through the prayers of anyone else on the ministry team. This helps people to look to God as their healer rather than to the advice/help of another human being. Sometimes God begins a work at a conference that He intends to continue in the local church where a continuing relationship with a particular person on the pastoral prayer ministry team may be important. This may be appropriate in the local church but we shouldn't encourage it at conferences.

- If you find yourself 'out of your depth' in a particular prayer encounter, don't hesitate to ask for help from someone else with more experience.

It is amazing what God will do when believers come together in large numbers and are unified in worship. At the annual New Wine conferences we have witnessed many people receive the breakthrough in healing they have been longing for. The following are two brief examples:

Released from pain

One person who came to the conference had a rare heart
defect known as a myocardial bridge. There is no treatment for this, other than for the symptoms. About two
months before our summer conference their symptoms
became more severe and they would wake up with a
crushing pain in their chest which would worsen
throughout the day. This was both scary and debilitating. During an evening service, this person determined
that they would only go forward for prayer if someone
had a word of knowledge relating to their problem. That
word of knowledge came and they went forward for
prayer. Although they felt nothing special happen (and
went to bed that night assuming nothing had happened), it took a while for them to realise the next morning that the pain had gone. Wondering whether this was
a coincidence, they waited to see if the pain would
return before 'accepting' their healing. But as I write,
many months have passed since they were prayed for
and they are busy resuming all the activities in life the
sickness had forced them to curtail.

Chains broken

A lady wrote to us to tell us of her healing from bulimia
and bi-polar depression – illnesses she had suffered
from for more than ten years. She had arrived at the conference feeling terrible and struggling both emotionally
and physically. At that time she was receiving treatment
at a clinic for eating disorders and taking medication for
depression.

　　At one evening meeting a word of knowledge was
given regarding the issue of 'control' in someone's life.
This lady 'suddenly' found herself at the front, lining up

for prayer. She hadn't intended to go forward for prayer, but God had other plans. Whilst being prayed for, she felt overwhelmed by God's love for her and had a clear picture of chains being broken. She left the meeting that evening feeling happy and hungry! A friend bought her some chips and she tells of eating 'guilt free for the first time in years.'

Although in her heart she felt she had been healed completely, she wisely waited until her doctors had confirmed it to be the case. After six months of exhibiting no signs of an eating disorder and her moods remaining stable she was signed off by the hospital and it was at this point that she wrote to tell us of what God had done. In her letter she said, 'Doctors have confirmed both healings and I've been amazed at how alive I've felt. God is awesome. Giving control over and trusting in Him was the final step in starting a new life as a whole person.'

In the Community

In the days of the early Jerusalem church the whole community brought their sick for healing and some exceptional things were happening.

> 'As a result, people brought the sick into the streets and laid them on beds and mats so that at least Peter's shadow might fall on some of them as he passed by. Crowds gathered also from the towns around Jerusalem, bringing their sick and those tormented by evil spirits, and all of them were healed.' (Acts 5:15–16)

Healings were not confined to those who were already Christians. Some were healed and then subsequently gave their lives to Jesus Christ as Saviour and Lord.

Similarly, in our generation, this ministry should not be confined to within the walls of our church buildings and the community of the converted. We remember that 'The meeting place is the learning place for the market place.' The Church needs to have both a model for healing which is easy to use outside the church building and a renewed confidence to minister healing anywhere and everywhere we go: our homes, our places of work, the school gate, our social clubs, trains, planes, and even the supermarket – all are places where, during the course of natural conversation, we can offer to minister healing to anyone who is sick. John Wimber used to insist, 'The meat is in the street.'

Not long ago an Iranian man came to us for prayer on the streets. He came somewhat reluctantly, urged by his friend who told him, 'It can't do you any harm!' The man was in some pain, but wasn't precisely sure what his problem was – he had either seriously pulled some muscles or cracked a rib – but he had a pain down the left side of his upper body. The team prayed for him and moments later he looked up in shock as the pain left him. He was jubilant and began waving his arms up and down, exclaiming, 'The pain has really gone!' His friend merely commented, 'See, I told you it would!'

Recently, some members of our congregation took healing on the streets a step further and began a 'healing in the pub' initiative. This stemmed from one couple attending a local pub. One night they noticed it was advertising a 'psychic healing evening', so they approached the landlord and asked if a group of Christians could hold a healing evening. The landlord agreed and so an evening was arranged and subsequently advertised in the pub.

On the first evening, a small group introduced themselves as being from the local church and said they would go from table to table and pray for anyone who was sick. A group of lads at one table began making fun of them, but after they had got past the joking one of them said quite seriously that he had a pain in his neck so the team prayed for him. Normally, it would be common to lay hands on the affected area, but the lady who was praying felt to place her hand over the young man's heart and found herself praying that God would heal his heart too. Another of the lads spoke up and said, 'How do you know that? He's just broken up with his girl-friend and he's completely gutted about it.' She replied that God had prompted her to do it. After she had prayed the pain left and the young man's neck was healed.

One of the reasons for the growth of the early church was the remarkable healing ministry that was happening and we read that, *'The Lord added to their number daily those who were being saved'* (Acts 2:47). Around the world today, where churches are rediscovering the healing ministry and elevating it to its rightful place alongside the teaching, evangelistic, prophetic and pastoral ministries of the church, they too are experiencing steady growth. God adds to their number those being saved. Moreover, instead of being cynical the young man began a serius conversation about God.

If healings were taking place both in our local churches up and down the country and in the communities served by those churches, then there would surely be a stirring in the nation. These healings will happen if church leaders and members alike commit themselves to seeking the presence and power of the Lord of glory and if they are willing to rediscover and pursue the ministry of Jesus as outlined earlier in this book.

A church leader recently made a comment to this effect:

'Signs and wonders occur on the frontier between the kingdom of God and the dominion of darkness. If you are not seeing signs and wonders, ask yourself if you are any longer on the frontier.'

I pray that as you commit yourself and your church to living 'on the frontier' you will have the joy of seeing God at work in healing those to whom you minister, and also the privilege of being part of a Church which is continually growing in numbers to the glory of God.

About the Author

John and Anne Coles took over the leadership of New Wine from David and Mary Pytches in 2001. They are based at St Barnabas in Finchley, North London. They led the church for twenty years, seeing it develop from small beginnings into a vibrant multi-cultural church. John is now the Director of New Wine. Anne is the ministry pastor at St Barnabas, having been the worship leader through the transition from choir-led to contemporary band-led worship. She has overall responsibility for developing New Wine's women's conferences.

Contact Information

New Wine Networks
c/o St Barnabas Church
Holden Road
London
N12 7DN
Tel: 020 8343 6130

New Wine Trust
4a Ridley Avenue
Ealing
London
W13 9XW
Tel: 020 8567 6717
Email: info@new-wine.org